THE

HISTORY OF IDEAS

The
History of Ideas

AN INTRODUCTION

GEORGE BOAS

CHARLES SCRIBNER'S SONS · *New York*

A–1.71 [C]

Printed in the United States of America
SBN684-71714-X
Library of Congress Catalog Card Number 74–85278

TO TOM TASHIRO

Preface

The purpose of this book is to set forth as simply as possible some of the major problems that confront the historian of ideas. Work in this field is relatively new. The History of Ideas Club at the Johns Hopkins University, founded by the late Professor A. O. Lovejoy, Professor Gilbert Chinard, and the undersigned, united a group of scholars in 1923, one of the most eminent of whom is Marjorie H. Nicolson. But W. F. Albright, the archaeologist; Ludwig Edelstein and Harold Cherniss, classicists; Bentley Glass, the biologist; Owsei Temkin, historian of medicine, along with a younger generation of scholars, all cooperated in making the Club a monthly meeting place where some of the ideas discussed in this book were illuminated and analyzed. In 1940 *The Journal of the History of Ideas* began publication with a distinguished editorial board and

Philip P. Wiener as managing editor. It is safe to say that under his guidance the *Journal* has been the source of some of the most important work in intellectual history now going on. Universities have begun to develop departments of the history of ideas and it looks as if the field would continue to be cultivated as part of the standard curriculum in the liberal arts. An introduction to this study then would seem to be useful.

That I should be the man to write this introduction might be questioned. My excuse is that for forty years I have done little else than write articles and books within this area. That in itself is not proof of competence and it may well be that critics will find the chapters which follow deficient in one detail or another. It would indeed be strange if they did not. I have no pretensions to writing a definitive treatise on this subject. It is an introduction and does not aim to be anything more.

The person who would study the history of ideas must have a kind of curiosity about the human mind and its workings that is not common. He must be willing to treat ideas that seem silly or superstitious and that are perhaps obsolete with the same care as he would give to established truths. For the history of ideas tells us among other things how we got to think the way we do—and if that is not of importance, one wonders what is. He must also poke about in odd corners, for ideas are quicksilver in the way they roll about and turn up in places where logic would never have pushed them. Above all he must be patient about historical causation and not commit himself either to materialism or to spiritualism while he is writing. If he is willing to indulge in a kind of benevolent skepticism, he will write in all probability a book that will be more enlightening than one written from the point of view of some special philosophy of history. Philosophies of history, like all philosophies, may be beautiful structures, but they have a way of getting mixed up with facts. One who is subject to their charm is likely to find what ought to have been rather than what was. I shall be told that I, too, have a philosophy of history, and the charge is inescapable. I have one. It recognizes the real existence of chance and is willing to settle for the probable and not seek the absolutely true. It also assumes that the human mind is an active force in the course of history and not an inert patient upon which economic, erotic, or even social causes operate.

It will be noticed that this book has two parts. The first part needs no explanation, but the second contains three historical sketches which, I hope, will illustrate some of the problems of intellectual historiography. The first, on the idea of *The People*, is intended to show how a very influential idea contains ambiguities, both descriptive and normative, that are often concealed. The material in it is drawn for the most part from a larger study of the same idea called *Vox Populi*. The second sketch, *Monotheism*, tries to suggest how two distinct ideas coalesced into one, the two ideas being that of the religious and that of the metaphysical God. The third sketch, on the idea of *The Microcosm*, deals with something which is obsolete except in one of its phases. The idea involved was used to bring intellectual harmony into the cosmos, and though it was never a major idea in European history, it had a certain influence in religious and literary circles.

My debts to others are so numerous that I cannot attempt to list them. But I think that I owe more to the men and women who have followed my courses both at Johns Hopkins and at Santa Cruz than to any single person other than A. O. Lovejoy. Had he lived, he would have seen the flowering of the tree of the History of Ideas he planted so many years ago and would have rejoiced at its vigor. But even he, fertile thinker that he was, learned from his pupils as we have all learned from him.

Special acknowledgment is made to Mrs. Elizabeth Wrenn Houston for her rendering of the Tree on Sephirot.

G. B.

Ruxton, Maryland 1968

Contents

PART ONE

·1·

What Is the History of Ideas?

The first problem which a historian of ideas has to face is, Just what am I writing the history of? For few words are as ambiguous as the word "idea." By latest count it had twenty-five meanings. Of these the two most frequent are "that which is known" and "that which is perceived," both of which derive from the original Greek. For centuries philosophers have said that we know only ideas, and others have gone further to say that we know only our own ideas. The followers of John Locke called colors and sounds ideas, and when it was believed that such sensations arose in the brain after certain sensory nerves were stimulated by light rays or air waves, then these sensations (or ideas) were said to have no duplicates in the world of other people and things. They were as private as dreams.

When the word "idea" referred to that which is known,

it denoted (1) something that might be true or false, such as a declarative sentence, a proposition, an assertion, and (2) an object, or a person, a work of art, an historical event. For instance, we say that we know that Washington was the first President of the United States, that 2 plus 2 is 4, that San Francisco is west of New York. But this does not mean that we know in the second sense of that word George Washington, or 2 plus 2, or San Francisco, or New York, It would be better to say that we know about them. We know about them and what we know may be true. If it seems strange to say that we do not know 2 plus 2 when we do know that the sum is equal to 4, that is because the second meaning of "know" does not apply to such things. It is nonsense to say that one knows 2; one knows something about it.

In another sense of "know," we can also say that we know the works of Giotto, meaning that we have seen them and can possibly recognize them; that we know San Francisco in the sense that we have been there and seen what there is to see there, the hills, the cable cars, the harbor, the parks, the museums. We also know our friends, meaning that we have first-hand acquaintance with them. But to know something in this sense is not the same thing as to know about it. To have a friend who on given occasions has been kind, truthful, amusing does not permit one to say that he is always kind, truthful, and amusing, but merely that when you have been with him he was so. That is why two people who know the same man, the same work of art, the same city, may disagree violently about them. We tend to objectify our ideas of things and cancel out whatever contribution we ourselves make to our experiences. So far we may say that we may have ideas-of and ideas-about. The former always are of particular things, persons, or events; the latter, of classes of them. The two kinds of knowledge have been called immediate or direct knowledge, acquaintance, appreciation, and even enjoyment, on the one hand, and mediated, indirect, descriptive or inferential knowledge, on the other. They correspond in other languages to *cognoscere, connaître, kennen,* and to *scire, savoir,* and *wissen* respectively. It is too bad that we cannot use two words in English for two different experiences, and much punning in epistemology would have been spared us if it had been possible. But we have to make the best of our linguistic limitations as of all others.

There is unfortunately a further complication that a historian of ideas must untangle. Sometimes what one knows is a matter of fact, sometimes a matter of policy. To know that the earth is an oblate sphere is to know a fact. To know that freedom of speech should not be abridged is a matter of policy. Ideas of fact are always expressed by the verb "is" or "is not"; ideas of policy by "should" or "should not." One is not likely to dispute the fact, once it is known, that the 18th Amendment was repealed by the 21st; but one can still debate the wisdom of the repeal if one wishes to. The distinction between the two sorts of ideas is not absolute, for policies are conditioned by facts. It is, for instance, assumed by most debaters that the proponents of a policy have the burden of proof on their shoulders. And the proof of a policy may be said to be based on the truth of three propositions of fact: (a) there are evils in the present system; (b) the proposed policy will eliminate them or greatly reduce them; (c) the proposed policy will not introduce new evils. To prove these three propositions is not a light task, for there are always evils in every situation and the very fact of change is felt to be evil by some people. "Let well enough alone," "Let sleeping dogs lie," "Sufficient unto the day is the evil thereof," and their equivalents are the usual rules by which people who dislike change will be guided. Furthermore, a question of policy cannot be decided unless one knows whether the facts permit its realization. The pursuit of happiness is a natural right expressed as inalienable in the American Declaration of Independence. But though one may believe this, sooner or later the fact dawns upon one that some men find their happiness in destroying other peoples' and the additional fact that happiness is an end the means to which are frequently unavailable. Every undergraduate would probably like to graduate with honors, just as every contestant in a competition would like to win the prize. There is no need to point out that the facts prevent the realization of such dreams.

Just as policies are conditioned by facts, some propositions of fact have been conditioned by policies. This does not always appear at first sight. It took, for instance, about two hundred years for the Copernican theory to be generally accepted. Why? Because it contradicted the Bible. Joshua could not command the sun to stand still if it was not moving. Here the conditioning policy was the belief that everything stated in the Bible must be absolutely, literally, and eternally true. This could be rephrased as, "We should believe everything that is stated in the Bible, whether matters of fact or of policy." Now there may be an objection here on the ground that I am talking about our beliefs and not about the facts. That is true. But our subject is the history of ideas, and ideas that no one believes in can hardly figure in history. If one is inclined to use the word "knowledge" to mean "ideas which are incontrovertibly true," that is possible. But such a definition would not fit our needs. For what is incontrovertibly true has no history. It simply subsists and may not even be known.

Not only may ideas be of fact or of policy, but they may also be, as William James, Josiah Royce, John Dewey, following Charles S. Peirce, pointed out, plans of action. They are ideas of something that is intended, which, it is hoped, will be realized in the future. They thus are allied to ideas of policy. An inventor, for instance, has the idea of a machine; the writer, of a novel; the political reformer of a better social order. These ideas resemble ideas of policy in that they are "of" nonexistent things, but they are usually made to fulfil a policy already accepted. They are very rarely mere fantasies or dreams. We can assume, for instance, that a man will know to begin with that a given state of affairs is bad; too many children catch polio; too many families are badly housed; too many international disputes are handled with ammunition. How many is "too many" will always be subject to debate. But once agreement is reached on that, a policy will be formulated to correct the evil, to reduce it, or to eliminate it. But a policy is not a plan of action. Two people may agree that something should be done and also agree that the evil in question has always existed and always will exist. It has been argued, for instance, that though war is an evil, it cannot be eradicated since men have always fought, being aggressive animals. Fighting, we are told, is nature's way of proving biological superiority. Others will argue that evil must exist as a challenge to the man of virtue, not something to be annihilated, but something to be lived with, to be borne with equanimity. Such ideas belong to the history of ethical theories.

Assuming, however, that a policy has been accepted, one then has to frame a plan of executing it. This plan is an idea in the third sense of the term and might better be called an ideal. It may vary from the precision of an engineer's or an architect's drawing to the vagueness of social reform. And since it does not correspond to anything that exists external to the mind, that is, to any fact, it cannot have truth in the ordinary sense of that word. It may turn out to be good or bad, efficient or wasteful, satisfactory or disappointing. But in all probability a plan when carried out will be good in the eyes of some and bad in the eyes of others. People differ not only anatomically but temperamentally. Not only do their tastes differ, but their interests also, and it is almost impossible to change the state of affairs without treading on someone's toes. Such interests are best exemplified in the lobbies in Washington, the fourth power in the body politic. In 1962 it was clear that something should be done to prevent reckless and murderous men from buying firearms by mail. It was also proposed that all firearms be registered. But enough pressure was brought to bear upon Congress to prevent any bill from being passed which would enact such measures.

Almost every idea, whether of fact or policy or a plan of action, carries an emotional charge. The simplest idea of fact may be extremely pleasant or unpleasant. I think it was St. Bernard who suggested that a man given to erotic fantasies should think of a woman with her skin removed. But the pictures in medical encyclopedias of the gross muscular system are far from repulsive to physicians, though few men would find them as seductive as the external anatomy. The sight of a gnarled and sterile apple tree may seem charming to a lover of the picturesque and revolting to an orchardist. Mathematicians are said to find their ideas aesthetically pleasing, and the late Edna St. Vincent Millay announced that Euclid alone had looked on beauty bare. And apparently beauty is more beautiful bare than clothed. In short, one can become as pleased or displeased by a statement of fact as by a statement of value. It will be recalled that one of the criticisms of naturalistic novels, those of Zola, Gissing,

and Dreiser, was that they dealt with "unpleasant subjects." From the scientific point of view, no subject is any
more pleasant or unpleasant than any other. Yet even
a word, not what it names, can be unpleasant. And some
words in themselves are considered to be noble or edifying
or even sacred. Nothing would seem at first sight to be
less emotionally loaded than the word "nature." Yet comments upon what it names run from its bloody fangs and
claws to its spiritual and uplifting character: "One touch
of Nature . . ." One never knows before examination
when simply reading or hearing a word whether it names
just the factual side of an idea or its normative side. The
very word "idea" for that matter has given rise to
"idealist," and an idealist may be either an impractical
dreamer or a spiritual guide.

It is this aspect of ideas that the late Arthur O. Lovejoy
called "metaphysical pathos." Even very abstract terms
like "unity," "eternity," "immutability," or their con-
traries, too, "variety," "the dynamic," "vitality," "creativity," to some people suggest a very high value, regardless of what is unified, eternal, unchangeable, being
created, and so on. We used to read, until about the middle of the nineteenth century, of steadfast characters,
everlasting beauty, national unity, but the fashion
changed and we began to hear of dynamic personalities,
creative artists, multiversities, national diversity, all of
which was written in eulogistic tones. The historian of
ideas must, then, be keenly aware of the metaphysical
pathos of the language used by the writer whom he is

studying. For it is that which at times determines what ideas will be entertained and how far they will spread. The word "nature," to which I have referred, and its derivatives have been shown by Lovejoy to have sixty-six meanings. But the writers who used the words and phrases involved never recognized the ambiguities which gave their language its persuasive force.

Yet the history of ideas is not confined to historical semantics. The history of words, as given for instance in the *New English Dictionary,* is extremely useful, for it not only dates the first use of a meaning but also shows the changes in time as they occur. It suggests but does not describe how a primitive idea proliferates and evolves into new ideas and it gives one a fairly reliable clue to when this happens. But a dictionary aims only to give the meaning of words, not of ideas, and sometimes a single idea may have two names. This frequently happens in English where there is often a choice between a Latin and an Anglo-Saxon derivative. Should we speak of breathing or of respiration? Similarly the People, the Populace, the *Plebs,* the Mob, the Multitude, *Hoi Polloi* and a few other terms, have all been used interchangeably and no one to date has been precise about just who was being referred to. Sometimes, of two words with the same denotation, the connotations vary, one being "proper," the other indecent. Sometimes a given word is called poetic in the dictionaries and another is called vulgar or colloquial. Sometimes words have changed their meaning radically and two words with antithetical meanings have taken each other's place. Thus "subjective" in the seventeenth century and the Middle Ages meant what we mean today by "objective" and "objective" meant what we mean by "subjective." Perhaps enough has been said now to show that dictionaries are very useful for informing us about the history of words but that such a history is not a history of ideas.

The history of ideas, moreover, is not the history of a science or a philosophy. Sciences and philosophies are clusters of ideas, each of which has it own history. Physics, for instance, began as a collection of simple recipes for weights and measures out of which in due course certain general principles emerged. These general principles became organized into that branch of physics known as statics. Within the fields of cosmology and statics were certain ideas related to the composition of material bodies, supposed to be made up of various parts of "the elements" —earth, water, air, fire—or, of course, of one element alone. By the time of Aristotle each of the four elements had what he called its natural position, earth being at the center of the universe, water above earth, then air above water, and above them all fire. By this time dynamics was added to statics and so bit by bit new problems arose within the original set of problems, which, as they were solved, were called physics, or the science of natural things. A science then is that set of related problems which have been solved at some given time. None have ever been solved to the satisfaction of all succeeding generations, but as long as one is solved to the satisfaction of the scientists at a certain date, nothing more is required.

All sciences use methodological rules, the rules of logic in the old fashioned sense of "correct thinking," and general principles such as "nothing is made from nothing," the causal principle (no effect without a cause), the principle of the uniformity of nature, and a number of others which sound like descriptions but are really procedural rules which (like the rules of chess or poker) determine in part the nature of the game. One can of course write a history of astronomy or physics or chemistry, but the historian of ideas would be more likely to write the history of the principle *ex nihilo nihil* or of the idea of universal determinism or of the concept of experimentation, which are ideas found in common in several of the physical sciences as well as in several of the quasi- and pseudo-sciences. Similarly, a man trained in philosophy might write a history of the idea that the world is a rational structure—or of the antithetical idea—as Lovejoy wrote the history of the idea of the great chain of being and W. F. Albright the history of monotheism in his *From the Stone Age to Christianity*. Monotheism is obviously more or less confined to the realm of theology, but it is part of the vast idea or intellectual goal of finding unity where undisciplined observation sees only multiplicity. The great chain of being was found first in a dialogue of Plato (*Timaeus*) as a philosophic idea, but it spread into biology, literary criticism, theories of history, and indeed it became almost ubiquitous.

The curious way in which an idea flows out of its field of origin into other fields is a special subject of the history of ideas. Take as an example the Law of Contradiction which is usually thought of as essentially a logical principle. We accept it without question when we are thinking, or at least when we are criticizing someone else's thinking. A debater looks sharply at his opponent's argument to see whether he has contradicted himself. In the courtroom a lawyer cross examines a witness to see if he can be caught in self-contradiction. It is assumed that the facts can be expressed in logically consistent terms. The model for this is geometry. Given the axioms, definitions, and postulates, all the theorems ought to be internally coherent. But geometry does not describe the world of space and time. That world can be made to approximate what geometry demands of it by a sort of purification. That is, one can make edges which are almost straight, wheels which are almost circular, but one always has to allow for the deformation caused by the materials with which one is working: wood, paper, pencils, etc. If geometry can be thought of as the perfect model of a mathematical system, then one can divide one's ideas into those that are mathematical and those that are historical. The latter are the ideas about what takes place here on earth in space and time.

The perfectly consistent ideas of mathematics are able to be consistent because they pertain to a world in which there is by definition neither change nor matter, hence no variety within a class nor growth within an individual.

What Is the History of Ideas?

Once a mathematical concept is defined, it stays put. But this is clearly not the case with historical beings. Their temporal dimension alone suffices to indicate change within them. The descriptions of a baby, for instance, seldom apply accurately to the man into whom he grows. And on a larger scale, what can be said about the birth of a nation does not apply to its later years. Colonial America was hardly the United States of the middle twentieth century, though there are of course some descriptions which apply to both—for instance, the language generally spoken then and now. But such descriptions are usually trivial. What can be said that is true of both the acorn and the oak? Of the marble and the statue? Possibly the material out of which they are made. But neither the statue nor the oak is merely matter on the level of human experience.

In spite of this, the Law of Contradiction has been taken out of its logical context and applied to matters of human behavior. One must not only learn to tell the truth but to act consistently as well. Consistency of character became both an ethical ideal and an aesthetic rule for novelists and playwrights. As early as Aristotle, consistency of character was held up to the dramatist as essential to a good play. Horace in his *Ars poetica* popularized the notion. Let Achilles be always Achilles is the favorite way of putting this rule. But Achilles was not always Achilles in his real life. No one is always anything. We vary from situation to situation, and both Aristotle and Horace must have known this. In fact the former wrote a couple of books to tell people how to behave consistently. The recipe was: Follow the Golden Mean. He realized that consistency of behavior was an ideal, something to be hoped for, not something ever to be observed in real life. Why was it laid down as an ideal?

The answer is that consistency of character has practical value. First, it helps others to understand your behavior, to anticipate what you are likely to do, to obviate senseless irrational conduct. Still this is not identical with the logical principle from which it arose. But it treats human beings as if they were mathematical concepts, and that is what the sciences have to do with all their subjects. Otherwise the world would never rise above the higgledy-piggledy disorder of raw experience. To understand is to uncover the order that is supposed to reside concealed in disorder. If the ancients were able to clarify all material substances by grouping them under the heads of the four elements, it was because they thought that all things behaved in one of four different ways. And if we today group all material things under one hundred and four names, that is because we have a different and less obvious way of classifying them. We accept the theory of elements and compounds, and the elements are distinguished by their atomic numbers. We still have solids, liquids, and gases, but within each of these three groups we make further differentiations. But in spite of all these distinctions, we expect the members of each group to behave in predictable ways. We treat them as if they were rational concepts, not things. Which is all that we can do if we wish to have a consistent science.

There is a further change when we observe that the ethical or psychological applications of the rule of consistency may cause emotional disturbances that are thought to be socially undesirable. It is possible that men would be happier if it were admitted that they might change in accordance with the situations in which they find themselves. They do so change, as we all realize, but that makes things hard for the psychologist who would like to be rigidly scientific. In a laboratory one can arrange situations which are almost constant. But we do not live in laboratories. Hence we try to follow a rule, either a rule of ethics or of etiquette.

The historian of ideas would like to know how a logical principle became a guide for behavior. It is possible—though improbable—that the Greeks had a more stable culture than we have. If so, consistency of character would have been more normal than it is in our more heterogeneous society. On the other hand, ideals are seldom reflections of what exists.

The history of ideas, moreover, is not literary criticism. No poem, play, or novel has ever been any the better for incorporating recognizable ideas. Nor would it be any the worse for not incorporating them. Most critics, for instance, are agreed that Shakespeare's sonnets are very beautiful, but the ideas they express are trivial for the most part. On the other hand, Tupper's *Proverbial Philosophy* is given a very low rating by literary critics and yet is a mine of generally accepted ideas. This caveat ought to be unnecessary, but unfortunately some writers have seemed to think that historians were attempting to praise a literary work when they were discussing the ideas that appeared in it.

By a peculiar kind of interpretation one can say that an adventure story contains the idea of all escape literature, that it urges its readers to become hoboes or explorers or big-game hunters or highwaymen or something of that sort. Or again, by a similar technique one could say that *Othello* was an anti-Moorish drama and *The Merchant of Venice* anti-Semitic. If a novel has its serious characters from the upper social classes and its comic from the lower, then one could say that its author was identifying the serious and the comic with social rank. This was in fact a tradition in Renaissance literary aesthetics, for though the lower classes might be good, they were always quaint, picturesque, or just funny. But after all, most of our virtues come from the customs of the ancients, by which courage, chivalry, generosity, honor were esteemed above endurance itself. Yet it is true that the notion of a classified society is present in most contemporary novels; society would not have had classes if egalitarianism had been practiced as well as preached. This is a truism.

Similarly one should not confuse the history of ideas with mind-reading, psychoanalysis, or even the sociology of knowledge. The historian who seems to know by intuition what an author's intentions are is a mind reader. An author's intentions are simply his works. There is no standard lexicon of "Freudian symbols" that encode a man's ideas. Freud himself emphasized this and maintained that each patient has his own problems and his own suppressed desires and his own way of satisfying them. There seems to be little profit in reading unconscious motivation out of an author's words; that is the business of a trained psychiatrist. Ideas, after all, exist on the conscious level and their history has to stay on that level. It would undoubtedly be interesting to know why certain types of idea appeal to one man and not to another. But as of today the necessary information is lacking. One cannot psychoanalyze a dead man (though Freud tried to psychoanalyze Moses and Leonardo da Vinci), and whatever conjectures we may make about a dead person's motives, his sincerity, or his subjection to various influences are conjectures and nothing more. If the day comes on which psychoanalysis is applicable to groups rather than only to individuals, then we shall have the data which will help us to determine why a man thinks as he does. Similar comments must be made about the sociology of knowledge. The discipline is still very young and, though it promises well, it has not yet reached the point that would be needed for the historian of ideas. Nevertheless, in view of the social determination of types of idea, as evidenced in religion, in art, and in economics —to limit ourselves to these—the sociology of knowledge may turn out to be a necessary adjunct to historical explanation.

So much for what the history of ideas is not. Now, what is it?

First, it is the history of beliefs, assertions of either fact or policy. Let me cite an example.

There is an old Latin proverb, *Poeta nascitur non fit* ("The poet is born, not made"). This has always stood for the idea that artistic talent is innate and cannot be acquired by training. You can, its proponents might say, teach a person the technique of an art, but beyond technical skill, virtuosity, lies aesthetic excellence, beauty. The plausibility of the idea is fortified by observation. Scores of painters, composers, poets practice their art at any given time. Some are very gifted technically. Yet out of a hundred contemporaries only a few emerge as masters. Mozart, Haydn, and Beethoven seem to be valued not because they never violated the rules of musical composition, but for other qualities which it is prudent to leave undefined. Similar remarks could be made about Delacroix, Géricault, Monet, and Picasso. The imagination, the inventiveness, the self-confidence of such artists seem to be congenital, something that might be strengthened by experience but hardly acquired from it. Hence the idea of congenital genius, *ingenium*, which seems more admirable than talent, which is learned. It is an instance of the supposed superiority of nature to art, of instinct to learning. If one were to trace the history of this idea, one would have to attach it to a form of cultural primitivism, to anti-intellectualism, to the arts of the savage and the peasant, to the cult of childhood.

I have already mentioned that peculiar feature of ideas

which is their overflowing into fields in which they did not arise. The superiority of nature to art again may be found in discussions even of religion, where the man who who is "naturally religious," the man who approaches saintliness, is sometimes felt to be inherently nobler than he who has found his religion in books. To undergo a conversion because of inner illumination would be thought of as better than to be convinced of a religious truth through argument. The former gives wholehearted real assent, to use Cardinal Newman's term, in his *Grammar of Assent*; the latter gives "notional assent." The Greek ethicists made much of the life according to nature, though they all disputed about what such a life would be like. The natural man would presumably know what was good by instinct. He would be like an animal in this respect, knowing without schooling what to eat and what not to eat, temperate in his lusts, modest in his needs, shunning superfluities. Similarly if one held to this idea, one would probably believe in the importance of something called self-expression, which, once more, might turn up as a goal or as the means to a goal in education, ethics, religion, or art. Just what the self and self-expression are is far from clear and we shall have occasion to play upon their obscurities later. But the sanctity of the self and its right, indeed its duty, to express itself is the more plausible the vaguer the ideas remain.

Each idea, as we have said, is likely to have both descriptive and normative aspects. "Nature" may refer to the subject matter of the natural sciences or to that which is contrasted with the supernatural or the unnatural (the abnormal). Sometimes the supernatural is thought of with awe, sometimes with contempt: with awe when the speaker is religious, with contempt when he is empirically minded. The unnatural is usually thought of as something bad, but sometimes it may be accepted as simply the unusual. "Art" again may simply mean that which is made or done by men rather than by God or nature, or it may distinguish those works or deeds which are especially praiseworthy. When one says that something is "really artistic," one usually means to praise it, not merely to say that it was made by a human being rather than spontaneously growing like a mushroom. At the same time, some paintings have been praised for being so naturalistic that they seemed real. Indeed, art as a faithful imitation of nature was an accepted slogan up to the present century.

Hence it is clear that before one can write the history of an idea one must disentangle it from all the ambiguities that it has acquired in the course of time. One must expect to find it appearing in contexts that vary from age to age. One must not be puzzled to find it used as a basis for praise and blame. To do all this requires very wide, indeed indiscriminate, reading, tolerance of inconsistency in a given man or book, and a willingness to accept wobbling from fact to value and from value to fact. In doing this, one is always tempted to quarrel with the men whose ideas one is discussing. This temptation is hard to avoid but nevertheless argument is not historical narration.

22

What Is the History of Ideas?

The Olympian objectivity which would be the ideal for the historian of ideas is seldom achieved. Indeed there is ground for thinking that it cannot be achieved, for if one is dealing with an idea that has stirred up men's souls, one is bound to have taken sides, to have shared to some extent in the emotions stimulated. It would be almost impossible to write an entirely objective history of the idea of popular government, of atheism, of communism, of art for art's sake, or even of progressive education. These ideas are programs of which most people either dislike or like some of the features intensely—and one would have to be as cold-blooded as a reptile not to have some feelings about their realization. Moreover if one also believed that all large-scale ideas were economically motivated, that each was held in the interest of some economic group, then no one could entertain such ideas except in his own interests, for everyone belongs perforce to some economic group whether he is aware of it or not. But this is also an idea whose history could be more or less clarified, and a historian has to make up his mind about its truth before he sets to work. Let me say for myself that this book is written from the point of view of one who believes—or assumes, if you prefer—that ideas may be held regardless of their relevance to economics or politics or religion; that they "make a difference" to the course of events; and that they sometimes are inferred from other ideas in a logical manner and do not always arise from nonintellectual sources.

· 2 ·

Basic Metaphors

There has always been a fundamental distinction made between literal and figurative speech. Yet I shall try to present reasons in this chapter for believing that even the simplest declarative sentence has an element of the analogical in it.

It must be granted that as far as words themselves go, some appear to be literal and others are either metaphorical or derived from metaphors. The names for animals and plants may be simply labels attached to them like baggage tags. They identify the objects about which we are speaking. So if we say, "That flower is a rose," no one is going to object that it is only a rose figuratively speaking. And if the rose in question has a name like Jaqueminot, Crimson Rambler, Silver Moon, the name selects the flower from a larger group into which the common noun "rose" has located it. But all these names are names of groups, classes, varieties of things, and none is like a proper noun which belongs to only one person, thing, or event: George Washington, My Fountain Pen, the War of 1812. Hence when one uses a common noun to identify something, one is saying in effect, "This thing before me has certain properties in common with other things." But these common properties are inevitably only some of the properties of the object about which one is talking. When, for instance, one says, "This is a rose," one overlooks its specific color—for it may be white, red, or pink—its fragrance, its texture, its size, its shape, and so on. All these vary. If one is a botanist and says, "This is a rose," one might be talking of an apple tree as well as of the garden rose, for the *rosaceae* are very numerous, having about two thousand species, and are found almost everywhere.

In ordinary conversation no confusion arises over such matters. We learn to pin certain labels on common things and we use them easily in communication. But it is well to remember precisely what we are doing. For every object can be labeled in a variety of ways. The way in which it will be named varies with the use to which one is going to put the information provided. We call this the context, but our purposes determine the context. We quickly catch the purpose by the social situation in which we find ourselves or because of the previous interests which have led up to the question now being put. There is no one answer, therefore, to the question, "What is that?" One guesses the type of answer that is sought and then gives the reply that is supposed to be "right." But after all, the interests of men are very numerous and only custom as related to social situations gives one a clue to the reference of a question.

If one is walking in a garden with a friend who owns it, and asks, "What is that flower?" clearly one wants the name of the flower. But the right answer might be, "That is a weed," or, "That is a flower I transplanted from my grandfather's garden," or, "That's grown from a cutting of that plant back there." One need only to think of all the possible kinds of question that can be asked to realize the vagueness of the general question.

Just what the literal, i.e., the etymological, meaning of the word used as a name may be we need not inquire. We are so habituated to our usual words that they do not puzzle us. But there are more metaphorical words in English than literal. One need but open a dictionary to be convinced of this. *Aardvark* is an earth-pig; *to abandon* is to place under jurisdiction; and *aberration* is a wandering away. When we say, "She abandoned herself to her grief," we do not consciously mean, "She submitted herself to the jurisdiction of grief," and if we do, then we have simply added metaphor to metaphor. The past participle "abandoned," used as an adjective means "profligate," "dissolute," "reprobate," each of which is a figure of speech. "Profligate" meant in Latin, "dashed to the ground"; "dissolute" meant "separated into one's parts"; "reprobate" meant to have been "put to the test" and presumably found lacking.

Most such words have lost their figurative meaning through use. For just as we speak of sunset and sunrise as if the sun moved and do so simply because we know that no one is going to take us seriously, so we use words like "abandoned" and "dissolute" and pay no attention to the etymological meaning. But there are, after all, times when a person is at a loss to find a word which says adequately what he wants to say and at such a time he resorts to an avowed figure of speech, an *as-if* (to use Vaihinger's term), a trope, a simile, a metaphor. Such a time may, of course, arise from simple ignorance or from the actual lack of a word. An example of this is the names that the American colonists gave the birds and flowers of their new country. They gave them the names of those birds and flowers of England which most resembled them. If they called the bird whose scientific name is *Turdus migratorius* (the migratory thrush) a robin, it was no doubt because, like the English robin, it had a red breast. This would be very misleading if we were not used to it. No one is bothered by calling *Helleborus niger* a Christmas rose, though it is not a rose and seldom blooms for Christmas. Such infractions of sense are to be expected, for words as time goes on take on new meanings whether these meanings are harmonious with the old ones or not. The first lesson a historian of ideas must learn is to expect the names of ideas to change and the ideas to spread.

The use of common nouns assumes the metaphysical doctrine of universals. Universals are supposed to be properties which can be embodied in a variety of places at one and the same time. They are called timeless, or eternal, for that reason. The clearest examples of universals are geometrical figures, which we learn at an early age are not identical with the diagrams that exemplify them. What is said about circles, triangles, and algebraic operations is supposed to be always true regardless of historical circumstances. We do not say that the sum of the angles of a plane triangle is 180 degrees in Baltimore during the month of July, but that the sum is 180 degrees always and everywhere. Yet if one took a protractor and measured the angles of a triangle drawn with a lead pencil on ordinary paper, their sum would not be exactly 180 degrees but 180 degrees plus or minus a small amount. However, the theorem in geometry is not about triangles drawn on paper. It is about ideal triangles which are not drawn anywhere. This comment on the idea of universals guides most of our thinking; yet it rests upon the interpretation of universals as *things*, immutable, unified, everlasting. Moreover, each universal is protected, so to speak, by an impenetrable frontier: nothing can get in or go out. If something is geometrically circular, then its circularity is free from any attack. It is *there*, unchanging, antihistorical, like a thing, a *res*, in its atomic nature, and like no material thing in its eternality. This obvious paradox has never prevented anyone from thinking in terms of universals and so far no substitute for them has ever been found, though statistics might have found a solution for the puzzle.

Things are a surrogate for universals. They too have

definite frontiers, presumably the surface at which they are touched. We think of the world as made up of these things, externally related to one another like eggs in a basket, stones on a beach, or molecules in the Brownian movement. We have injected these things below the level of observation, so that we think of atoms and whatever is inside the nucleus of the atom as if they too were things. The thing is enclosed in a hard shell and its "inner nature" is never thought to change. It was not until 1905 that anyone saw that the so-called natures of the chemical elements could change. For once a being was something, it had to remain that thing. Nothing could be both A and not-A at the same time and in the same respect, though not-A had to be what was felicitously called the contradictory of A, not the contrary. Hence a thing could be both red and sweet but it could not be both red and green at the same time and in the same place. The question of how one knew which adjectives were which is a difficult one, but attributes of a given class—color, taste, sound—might obviously be contradictories.

Such a term as "thing" got its meaning from the conditions of observation that date from prehistoric times. The naked sense organs perceive things only vaguely. The objects of vision change their size and shape as their distance from the eye grows greater. The objects of sound have no shape, but their intensity changes with distance and their pitch does also. Odors oddly enough fade out as one becomes used to them—or possibly as the olfactory nerves become fatigued. We can get the taste of an object only by coming into contact with it. And touch alone gives us evidence of the enduring qualities, the hardness and shape of the tactual object. It was probably this object that produced the notion of "thinghood" (*reitas*). In many cases the use of the word "thing" is metaphorical.

It cannot have escaped anyone's notice that there are events in the world as well as things. Events, occurrences, happenings, have a temporal dimension, best illustrated in growth in the animate kingdoms. Their temporal dimension can neither be telescoped nor be eliminated. The fact stubbornly confronts us that it takes time for a plant to grow out of its seed or a human being to grow out of a fertilized egg. Events can be handled by the symbolism of mathematics, but our ordinary linguistic symbolism is inadequate to the task. Hence we turn events into the symbolism of things and speak of them as if they had beginnings and ends and lateral frontiers. This presents difficulties to the historian who solves them by fiat, i.e., by a convention. The historians know that to date the American Revolution from 1775 is to lop it off from those revolutionary acts which led up to Lexington and Concord. Was the work of the Committees of Correspondence part of the Revolution? If so, how about the Boston Massacre (1770) and the Boston Tea Party (1773)? But all this was certainly in part caused by the Townshend Acts (1767). Then there were the Stamp Act of 1765 and the Sugar Act of 1764. But such matters are usually put into an introductory chapter, for otherwise one would retreat through the French and Indian Wars to the arrival of the first colonists in the Western hemisphere. So we speak of the American Revolution, the War of 1812, the Mexican War, the Civil War, and so on, and turn these strung-out events into things. We know that they are not things, but we are at a loss to know how else to deal with them.

A second metaphor, which is almost omnipresent, derives from, or at any rate is allied to, the process which I hesitatingly call *reification*. That is the figure of speech which says that a thing "has" properties, attributes, qualities, and that it is an agent which "does" this or that. When we say that the apple is red, we distinguish between the apple and its color, although there is no colorless apple. This practice has given rise to the old metaphysical puzzle of what would happen to the apple if we removed its color, odor, taste, texture, weight, shape, and so on. In other words, is a thing anything more than its properties?

We cannot settle this question here. But the very fact that it can be put shows that the questioner thinks it significant. A color, shape, odor must "belong" to something, he assumes. And in order to give them an owner, a subject has been invented, a thing, an It. That one cannot get at this subject except through its attributes does not disturb us. But the fact remains, nevertheless, that we may be arguing from grammar rather than from evidence. We use the demands of syntax as an ontological premise. When I was a schoolboy, we were told that no one knew what electricity was; one only knew what it did. We might have surmised that it was what it did.

The assumed subject is also found in impersonal verbs. No longer does anyone ask what *It* is that is raining or snowing. But at the same time we all have to say, "It is raining," and not simply, "Raining." Seemingly just as there has to be a subject which has attributes, so there has to be a subject to be the agent of all acts. Something has to do the raining, just as something has to do the thinking or the feeling. There have to be a wind to howl and a river to flow and light and sound to travel through space, for the howling and the flowing and the traveling are not enough. But again, no one has ever been able to distinguish between the wind and its howling or blowing or the river and its flowing or the light and sound and their passage through space-time. Yet these are more properly treated as events, not as things. But so powerful is the impression that behind all happenings there must be a thing that happens, that the ancients could make statues of Father Nile, of Boreas the north wind, of Apollo god of light. Though one cannot dogmatize about this, it is likely that the idea of agents for all acts is a projection into the external world of our own feelings of activity. If we make sounds, then all sounds can be refered to something like ourselves, but not entirely human. And so with all the other events with which we are familiar. And maybe the *It* which is the subject of the impersonal verbs goes back to some similar agent, a god.

Be that as it may, this usage is based on metaphor.

Basic Metaphors

Events occur *as if* they were the acts of an agent, human, nonhuman, superhuman, infrahuman. Attributes belong to a subject *as if* they were its property. As I distinguish myself from my eyes, ears, heart, and other organs, so do I distinguish myself from my clothes, my books, my friends. Hence I talk as if everything was a nuclear subject to be distinguished from its attributes. This verbal habit resembles the kind of animism that anthropologists used to say was the religion of primitive man. In that more or less fictitious religion every tree, every rock, every hill, was inhabited by a spirit whose acts were manifested in growth, in landslides, in earthquakes, and other natural phenomena. We have given up the belief in such resident spirits, but we still invest the things about us with the power to act.

The process of reification is to be seen even in ideas about historical events. Events like wars, economic changes (e.g., the Industrial Revolution), nations, artistic movements are all talked about as if they were substances concealed behind external appearances. We find writers asking what Romanticism really was, as if it were any different from what the Romanticists did. The spirit of a nation is assumed to be something permanent embedded in the nation's many changes. It is like the soul of a man, which was believed to have entered his embryonic body a few weeks after conception and to have stayed there until death. The spirit of America, the English character, the true German—all these are expressions of this figure of speech.

33

Similarly we see the same basic metaphor in the idea of times and ages. Sometimes the age is named after a ruler—Pericles, Augustus, Elizabeth I, Louis XIV. Sometimes it is named after its chronological position—Antiquity, the Middle Ages, Modern Times, each of which is said to have its own spirit. Sometimes an age is designated by some assumed cultural peculiarity—the Dark Ages, the Renaissance, the Enlightenment, the Age of Analysis, the Jet Age. In all such cases, the age is supposed to be almost homogeneous as far as its defining character is concerned. It is analogous to the characters described by Theophrastus: the Braggart, the Miser, the Slanderer, all of whom may act out of character from time to time but on the whole do not. So it would probably be admitted that some people in the Age of Reason were irrational and some poems in the Romantic Period were classical. Critics sometimes overlook the fact that Crabbe and Byron were contemporaries, that Delacroix and Ingres were contemporaries, that Beethoven and Clementi were also. But such people are said to be either "behind the times" or "born too soon." Since we are going to discuss the metaphor of ages below (Chap. 6), we shall cut off the discussion here at this point, contenting ourselves with simply pointing out that the spirit of an age is assumed to be existentially different from the people who live in an age.

A rational critique of the idea of ages and times as *things* to be distinguished from their contents leaves one wondering why anyone should ever have taken it seriously. The probable, though by no means certain, answer is that the idea of a thing carries with it the suggestion of unity and coherence plus that of stability. A thing or substance is like a rock which seems to endure, whereas an event is like a stream always flowing and never apprehensible. Unity, coherence, and stability have almost always been advanced as signs of value. The work of art which is unified and coherent has been held to be better than one which is diversified and incoherent. It will be called an "immortal masterpiece" which "posterity will cherish," one which "is not of today but for all time." Nations are praised for their unity of purpose, which may in the long run turn out to be pig-headedness and failure to adjust to new problems. Internal conflict is looked upon with as much horror as Americans look upon a diversity of political parties. The Catholic Church prides itself upon its immutable dogmas; it is *semper eadem,* always the same, and the tradition which is sacred, though apparently changing, is the exfoliation of what is already potentially present in Scripture. One can easily see that without the stability of the thing, one would be at a loss to know how to distinguish between acceptable and unacceptable changes. Reasoning demands, for instance, that no term in the course of an argument change its meaning. Similarly, when we think about or discuss religion, politics, art, ethics, or anything else that concerns human interests, we want our terms to remain steadfast. But steadfast though the terms may be, the things that they name will inevitably change—and we find ourselves in the situation of using old terms for new things.

For instance, we have the ancient Greek word *tragedy*. This word was defined in Aristotle's *Poetics* to describe, as he thought, the tragedies of the Greek poets. From his time on writers have written plays which continued to be called tragedies, some of which have been written in imitation of Greek plays, some of which were written to conform to Aristotle's definition, and some of which— Shakespeare's for example—were just written as their authors saw fit. Racine tells us in his prefaces what Greek playwright he was imitating and how he modified his original. Shakespeare and Marlowe tell us nothing; they simply give us their plays. Now it seems to be assumed that if *Death of a Salesman, Hamlet, Phèdre,* Seneca's *Hercules Furens,* and Euripides' *Trojan Women* are all tragedies, they must all be similar in some important respect, or that they all ought to be similar, or that they all conform to Aristotle's definition of tragedy or ought to. The fact that these plays were written by five different people in four different languages for five different audiences to be played in five different kinds of theater— assuming that *Hercules Furens* was a stage play and not a closet drama—should make them inevitably different. The trouble is that someone has called them all tragedies and therefore they must, regardless of what they actually are, be identical in their "tragic essence." The history of the word "tragedy" is not the history of the ideas that people have entertained about tragic drama. One could indeed write a history of this word. Similarly one could write a history of Aristotle's idea of tragedy, the way it was expanded by later writers, the way dramatists tried to exemplify it, what remained of it after the Renaissance, how Elizabethan dramatists challenged it by writing plays which they called tragedies and which did not conform to the Aristotelian canon, and how with the evolution of Western society new types of the tragic hero were incorporated into serious drama. A modern urban industrialized society will not have heroes who are tortured by the same kinds of guilt as Oedipus was, or Lear or Hamlet or Phèdre. But to write such a history would demand, above all, the precise definition of the idea, not the word, whose history was to be written. It is questionable whether the jealousy of God, the need for personal revenge, incest and its punishment, or for that matter insult, are any longer tragic motives.

One more example of how an old word is retained to name new ideas may not be superfluous. The word "democracy" is obviously Greek and means the rule of the *demos*, usually but unfortunately translated "people."[1] The *demos* was not all the people by any means. The word originally seems to have named certain districts of Attica and then came to mean collectively the native inhabitants of such districts. But when it was used in the compound noun "democracy," it might mean, as in Aristotle's *Politics* (1279b), the rule of the poor in their own interest. But since there are always more poor than

[1] The history of the idea of "the People" will be sketched below in Chap. 8.

rich people, it will also mean the rule of the many in their own interest. The poor, however, are not everybody, and a good state, says Aristotle, is one in which the interests of all are served. Hence he compares democracy to tyranny as a perversion of constitutional government.

In our own times the word has become so loaded with eulogistic connotations that almost any kind of government will be called democratic: constitutional monarchies like Great Britain, the Netherlands, Belgium, and the Scandinavian countries; republics like the United States, Mexico, and the Latin American countries; Communist states like the U.S.S.R. and the People's Republic of China, the German Democratic Republic and the Socialist Federated Republic of Yugoslavia, and so on. There is so little in common in all these republics and democracies that it reduces to the vague principle that they all serve the interests of *the People*. But the manner in which these interests are served in China is very different from the manner in which they are served in Great Britain. And so are the people who constitute *the People*. The fascism of Mussolini and the national socialism of Hitler were also said to exist to serve the interests of the Italian and German peoples. But *the People* in Germany were Germans who had less than one-eighth non-Aryan, i.e., Jewish, blood. *The People* in Italy were the major industrial corporations. What would be of interest to the historian of ideas is the development of the idea of who *the People* are and what religious, political, and even aesthetic rights they should have.

Basic Metaphors

The personification of *the People* is an example of a basic metaphor that has had increasing influence on the lives of Occidentals. It is metaphorical because it treats a heterogeneous collection of human beings as if they formed a homogeneous unity which could desire ends, have interests, speak, make contracts with other units or with ruling individuals. This imaginary person can have virtues, can be defended or attacked, loved, hated, feared, and despised. Yet at times *the People* have been only a part of the total population, and the least admirable part at that.

Here then are two examples of basic metaphors as they appear in the history of ideas. To them might be added those figures of speech used in scientific explanation, *purpose, cause, and universal regularity.* The very notion of a universe as a system of things and events such that all of its parts are describable in propositions which are logically consistent is a figure of speech, not a verifiable fact. It is probably needed as a rule guiding research, for if we were to admit inconsistency into our descriptions of nature, then anything might happen. In a similar manner Aristotle took as his guide, "Nature does nothing in vain," and Epicurus, *"Ex nihilo nihil."* Neither of these principles could be verified empirically and indeed no one has been quite sure of just what *ex nihilo* or *in vain* meant. *Ex nihilo* has sometimes meant that the effect must have previously existed in the cause and at other times simply that all events occur in a regular and predictable fashion. But just what Nature's purposes would be is unknown and unknowable and usually reduces, at least in Aristotle, to regularity. Since one of the aims of science is to systematize thought, and such principles or their equivalents are essential to the fulfillment of that aim, they will be retained and seldom submitted to analysis.

There is one very influential metaphor that cannot be omitted from this discussion. That is the figure of impressions. Impressions are literally something pressed into or stamped upon a yielding subtance. The standard substance, when the metaphor is used, has been wax. When the Greeks speak of sensory impressions, they are imagining that the human mind is like a wax tablet upon which impressions are made. This image is at least contemporary with Plato, for in *Theaetetus* (191-92) he discusses it. Some of the inferences drawn from this figure of speech were that the mind is always passive in sensation: the external world imprints its character upon the mind. Similarly, only material objects could be perceived, for the immaterial could make no impression on anything. Therefore something had to be invented to get the material object into the head so that it could act upon the brain. The followers of Democritus invented the *eidola*, which were little images of the objects that were constantly being sloughed off and whirling around in space; some of them hit the eye or, rather, a beam from the eye, like the light rays that we use nowadays. The impression had to be mental and exclusively mental, though it might look like the external objects from which it emanated. But some of them clearly did not look like them, the moon and its image for instance. When another assumption was made, that all knowledge is a compound of sensory impressions, it was inferred that one could know only one's own impressions and they were locked up in one's mind; that knowledge of the past and future, as well as of other people's minds, was impossible, for the past is over and done with and can make no impressions whatsoever and the future is not yet available to make any. And, though no one actually believed all this, it was argued on the basis of what was only an ill-fitting metaphor plus the assumption just mentioned, that one could know only one's self at the present moment—solipsism.

This seemed ridiculous to some thinkers, for it was a flagrant contradiction of common sense. Common sense is neither science nor philosophy but it serves to raise problems for both, and their answers must be made to square with it, within limits. What those limits are has never been made precise, but if physicists produced a theorem which said that one could push his fist through solid matter without breaking either the fist or the matter, no one would accept it as true. Light goes through solid matter and that is accepted—but we still maintain that solids are impenetrable. So when philosophers say that knowledge of the past is impossible, common sense rejects them. We just do not believe that we are shut up in our own skulls, though common sense associates the mind with the brain.

Yet we still speak of our impressions of people, places, and events. We speak of certain persons as impressionable. We urge people to "get out of themselves," as if they were self-enclosed. We ask children to be sensitive, as if all feelings were impressed upon them by external agents. Great men and great events are said to be impressive. A school of painting is called the Impressionists, and they recorded their impressions of things seen in the open air. And since impressions change with the changing light, one of them, Monet, recorded his impressions of haystacks, poplar trees, the façade of Rouen cathedral, water lilies at consecutive hours of the day.

Oddly enough, the fact of self-enclosure did not appear to be regrettable to some writers. On the contrary, it fitted in with another basic metaphor, that of inner natures. Things were thought of as being enclosed in a shell, and with no way of being reached without cracking the shell. Melancholy people liked the idea that no one could get at them; it gave them something to be sad about. They could complain about not being understood; they were elegantly solitary, like Mariana in the moated grange. A whole literary tradition grew out of this, the tradition of the lonely poet—usually in his garret. Poe is an excellent example of this. Since one is self-enclosed, the outer world is a gloomy mystery. Introspection is exercised because extraspection is impossible. There is perhaps no need to expatiate upon this any further.

Basic metaphors are required for thought. That must be granted. But metaphors should neither be mixed, if they are to serve intellectual ends, nor be inadequate. Mixed metaphors were used by the Metaphysical Poets and have recently come back into style for poetic purposes. That anything is really like anything else in other than in superficial ways is probably false. It would be safer to say that everything is an individual. But it should always be remembered that both science and philosophy are abstract and hence must not be replicas of perceptual experience. Raw experience is quite a different matter; it is a jumble of colors, sounds, and all the rest of the turning kaleidoscope of life. For that reason the conclusions of both science and philosophy will never quite fit raw experience. But one cannot remain on the level of raw experience if he is seeking to understand it, for the simple reason that understanding always transcends its object. Moreover, common sense has inner contradictions, as is noticeable in proverbial philosophy; and finally, if we accepted unenlightened common sense, we might also believe the earth to be flat.

· 3 ·

How Ideas Change

One might think that once an idea was established as true, it would never change. But only in mathematics has invariable truth ever been attained, and the eternal truth of mathematics is the truth of a formal logical system, not that of a single isolated theorem. Certain premises are laid down as postulates, certain logical rules of deduction are accepted, and the "truth" of any proposition signifies its consistency with the premises. It is of course assumed that no violation of the logical rules has been committed. Mathematical theorems are modified, refined, clarified, and sometimes reproved by demonstrations more elegant than those from which they were originally derived. But once they have been established, most people accept them without hesitation.

The kind of truth for which the ordinary man is looking is factual truth, not logical consistency. And most of our ideas are not parts of mathematical systems. Even when they are basic, like ideas about truth and falsity, good and evil, right and wrong, beauty and ugliness, they are questioned and often rejected or thoroughly revised. Whereas it was believed as late as the early nineteenth century that some truths are self-evident, it now looks as if the self-evident were simply the customary. Ideas become self-evident after they have been in circulation for a number of years. Ideas which when first pronounced seemed too horrible to be possible, now are accepted without a quiver. The Copernican theory, Freudianism, the Special Theory of Relativity—all were treated as fantastic when they were first broached. Now some of their vocabulary has entered into daily speech. Even ideas about good and evil have changed persistently during modern history. Who now would be willing to assert that the joy of the souls in Paradise is the sight of the damned screaming in agony in Hell? Yet such an idea was common up to the seventeenth century and was upheld by St. Augustine, St. Thomas Aquinas, and Peter of Lombardy.[1] It is an idea not unlike that expressed by Lucretius in the opening lines of the second book of his *De rerum natura*: "Sweet is it, when the winds are boiling the waves at sea, to watch the struggles of another man, safe on shore."

Who today would accept either of these thoughts? Again, who now believes that it is right to punish the

[1] D. P. Walker, *The Decline of Hell* (London, 1964), p. 29.

members of an offender's family for his offenses? As for ideas of beauty and ugliness, even ideas about the beauty of female nudes have changed, as may be proved by looking at any series of such paintings from the fifteenth century to our own time. It is safe to say that almost any idea, including mathematical ideas of numbers and space, has a history. One would like to know why.

But first one should know why men disagree. Aside from the pleasures of being different from other people and of sheer cussedness, there seem to be four main reasons for disagreement: (1) different definitions of terms; (2) the use of different information or authorities; (3) the acceptance of different premises; (4) different inferences drawn from the same premises.

1. Many arguments have ended with one of the antagonists exclaiming, "If that's what you meant, why didn't you say so at the outset?"

It would be convenient if people always defined their terms before starting to argue, but we all think that we use words in the standard way that is acceptable to all. When one thinks of words like "freedom," "art," "religion," "patriotism," and their derivatives, however, one realizes how seldom two debaters will agree on whether freedom is unlimited, whether the comic strips are art, where religion ends and superstition begins, and whether a conscientious objector is patriotic. Vagueness is the most abundant source of debate, and the debates that arise out of it are the most fruitless. Whether it is possible to attain perfect clarity of meaning this side of mathematics is questionable. For unless two debatable situations are exactly alike, no common noun or adjective will fit them both. But whether we can be perfectly clear or not, we can always hold such clarity up as an ideal.

Terms like sentences may have agreeable and disagreeable connotations. A conscientious objector may seem like a coward or a slacker to some men and saintly to others. The adjective "conscientious" is eulogistic, but the noun "objector" is pejorative, especially in the United States where objections and criticisms are considered bad form. Two people, therefore, might agree on a definition of conscientious objection and hold in reserve their bias. Hence if someone were to argue about the patriotism of a conscientious objector, violent disagreement might erupt, not because the debaters did not know what a conscientious objector was, but because they disagreed over the propriety of objections conscientious or not. The feeling that one ought to bow before the decision of the majority is not to be treated as base or unmanly or weak-kneed. The majority could be wrong, but some convention has to be accepted if peace within a society is to be preserved. On the other hand, there is a deep-seated feeling in some members of society that certain things are downright wrong, whoever orders you to do them.

2. In the second place no individual possesses all the information needed to settle any nonmathematical problem. People are as much differentiated by their schooling, their reading, their past conversations, as by their genes,

and it is the former that give them the information which they can bring to bear on any question. Here, for example, is a couplet which requires interpretation:

> To work a wonder, God would have her shown,
> At once, a bud, and yet a rose full-blown.

These are not very difficult lines and as soon as it is known that the woman referred to is the Virgin Mary, most of the difficulty disappears. But one must know that much. The only practical way to get this information is either to have already read it in, let us say, a college course in seventeenth-century English poetry or to have looked it up in a dictionary of quotations. But not even that tells the whole story, for the metaphor of the rose comes out of the Litany of the Blessed Virgin, which in turn is based upon the Song of Songs. If one finds the quotation in a dictionary of quotations, that is usually enough and one has the feeling that the authority is right.

It will probably be agreed that people differ both in the amount and in the quality of the information they possess. And if one is a historian of ideas, one never seems to possess enough. In fact this metaphor of Herrick's, which goes back to the *Song of Songs,* recurs in a somewhat different manner in the *Roman de la Rose* which was one of the most widely read and influential poems of the thirteenth century. The Rose in the first part of that poem stands neither for the Church nor for the Virgin, but for courtly love, and in the second part for physical love. In fact even in Greek the rose was a euphemism for a woman's *pudenda*. Suppose now that one was interested in tracing the history of the idea expressed in the Song of Songs 2:1: "I am the Rose of Sharon." One would have to know, first, what it symbolized according to the Hebrew commentators and, second, how it was reinterpreted by the Latin and Greek Fathers. The subsequent history of the verse and its meaning would involve one in a maze of research, and authorities might well be at odds because of the sources that they had used.

3. Among the fundamental ideas that come from authority are logical premises. People talk about the Oedipus Complex, heredity vs. environment, Marxism, the American Way of Life, the balance of power and the power vacuum, popular sovereignty, and they have only seldom examined the premises on which discussions of these ideas are based. They are all shorthand expressions for hypotheses, some of which have been well established, some poorly. But one cannot scrutinize every idea that swims into one's consciousness and has to have a place from which to start. Yet of two persons discussing, let us say, a boy's behavior, one may have taken as his premise the exclusive influence of heredity and the other that of environment. Hence one will say, "What could you expect of a boy whose grandfather was a notorious drunkard?" and the other, "His parents really ought to move out of that run-down neighborhood." If these two people were charged with the duty of improving the boy's behavior, it is obvious that they would be in complete

disagreement on how to do it or whether it could be done.

4. Sometimes—indeed frequently—two people may accept the same premises and draw different conclusions from them. For instance, in the second half of the nineteenth century people argued hotly about the implications of Darwin's theory of the origin of organic species. Two of the key terms in this theory were "the struggle for existence" and "the survival of the fittest." If an oversimplification will be tolerated here, two schools of thought emerged, both of which accepted both ideas. But one concluded that if the fittest would survive, there was little sense in building hospitals, mental asylums, schools for retarded children, or in fact most of our charitable institutions. Let the weak, obviously unfit, go to the wall. The other school, however, concluded that one of the factors that had helped the human race survive was the brain and that brain power was not always a factor of animal strength, and further, benevolence, mutual aid, and brotherly love were nature's ways of saving a species from extinction. In short, even if mankind was merely a natural animal, his total nature, not simply his nutritive and reproductive functions, must be included in an inventory of his character.

This is enough, I hope, to show how people disagree. To put the matter into its simplest terms, the experiences of people are very different.

If now one looks at experience as a whole, one will see five different aspects which might change the direction of our thoughts and thus give rise to new ideas.

How Ideas Change

1. *Perceptual objects.* By this I mean simply the sky, clouds, trees, stars, flowers, birds, houses, pictures, statues, costumes, with all their indefinite variety of colors, sounds, smells, tastes, textures. Out of this phantasmagoria of sensations and things, we pay attention to a restricted selection, sometimes based on those which are especially pleasant or unpleasant, very unusual, or curious. Perhaps a person calls our attention to some one thing or sensory quality, some particularly beautiful girl or some repulsively painted house. In any event, there is always a selection made either by our own interests or by those of someone else. A geologist would probably notice odd geological formations; a botanist some rare flower; a painter a remarkable combination of colors on a torn billboard. We are never aware of everything which we might be made aware of and it is improbable that of two people in the same perceptual field, both will notice— and remember—the same things.

2. *Their affective coefficients.* Very few perceptions are emotionally neutral, at least when new. They are in varying degrees either pleasant or unpleasant, though when we grow accustomed to them, they lose their affective color and we accept them calmly as they come and go. Yet much of conversation deals with our "feelings" about things and sensations, as it does about people and what they do and say and whether one likes them or not. The metaphysical pathos, to use A. O. Lovejoy's term, of an idea is its pleasantness or unpleasantness, and some ideas are so unattractive to some people that they seem inconceivable. Yet they are conceived. What might be called

the indifference of nature is a case in point. A father of six children, a loving husband, a virtuous citizen, is killed by a stroke of lightning. "It is downright unjust," someone remarks, "that such a man should be killed when vicious, cruel wasters are allowed to live." The author of such a reflection assumes that natural catastrophes should select their victims and kill off only undesirables. The indifference of nature to human standards of justice is thought of as a trait of Mother Nature, personified almost as a goddess. And since moral neutrality is hateful in human beings, so is it in gods. The emotional coefficient of the idea is in this case enough to lead people to believe in its falsity. Thus, when Freud's theory of infantile sexuality, Darwin's theory of the descent of man, Copernicus' theory of the sun's immobility first struck the European mind, their implications were not judged on the basis of their probable truth or falsity but on the horror which they inspired. It is probably fair to say that most of the ideas which seem "inconceivable" if they are not internally inconsistent, have repulsive overtones. I am thinking of "inconceivable" as equivalent to "too horrible to be borne."

3. *Memories.* Strictly speaking every experience of which we are aware is a memory by the time we are aware of it or talk about it. That is a matter for the psychologist to handle. It affects the historian of ideas only to the degree that it raises the problem of why out of thousands of impressions to which we might be paying attention we select certain ones and reject others. We know

that if a stimulus to perception persists continually, like the ticking of a clock, the noise of traffic, a strong odor, we soon become accustomed to it and we cease to be aware of it. We know also that a color or sound or odor or texture has to "stand out" from other sensations of the same type for us to be conscious of it. A square of black upon a background of black is not perceived unless its texture differs from the background, one or the other being rougher or smoother. A bouquet of flowers all of which are of the same variety has one consolidated odor, and the odor of each flower is not perceived unless one singles it out and sniffs it in isolation from the others. Furthermore, we usually perceive things from a certain distance, so that details which would be observed at close range are not seen. The grain of paper, the play of light on a flower, reflections of neighboring objects drop out of consciousness for the simple reason that they are not within the focus of attention.

Yet on the fringe there is a zone of possible experiences not beyond the range of perception like microscopic objects. On the contrary, we can see them if we wish, but we may not be interested in them. Why we are interested in having certain experiences and uninterested in others is again one of those psychological problems to which I have found no single answer. If all our experiences were consciously related to hunger or love or pride or self-assertion, the problem might be solved more easily. But the strength and the focus of these interests vary from individual to individual and usually there is a limit to their satisfaction. Even Don Juan must have calmed down between his sexual exploits, and the biggest glutton cannot continue to eat without interruption. Are the experiences between below the level of consciousness?

Whatever the cause of interest, its effect upon perception is clear. And when our memories come into play, they must count for even more in determining what part of our past life will be retained and what forgotten. If we are proud, we may retain both those experiences which bolster our pride and those which hurt it. But it will be noted that in most cases we maintain that we are the causes of the former and others of the latter. It is interesting that humiliating experiences of which we are ourselves the source more often occur in dreams than in waking life, whereas those of which we are the targets are more frequent in daily life. I venture to suggest— though this may tell more about me than about the human race in general—that more people are insulted in waking life than in dreams and more people feel they have behaved indecently in dreams than in waking life.

Whatever the reason, we spend a good deal of our time with our memories, dwelling upon them, gloating over some and shuddering over others, sorting them out, finding or inventing the causes of others, trying to learn from them in the expectation that experiences like them might recur. Among them are naturally things we learned in school or from reading or from conversation. A writer, even when not composing his autobiography, is recalling his past experiences—only he calls it his accumulated stock of information. But even if most of it is notes taken while reading or in the laboratory, they were jotted down after a careful selection; they fulfilled a conscious purpose. No two people can have exactly the same stock of information. There may be a high degree of consistency between them, but on the other hand, two men talking about the same book will often give conflicting reports. So two reporters of the same incident, two photographers of the same scene, two interviewers of the same man will differ in what they transmit to the public.

4. *Fantasies of the future.* A large part of our daily life is also taken up in hopes, aspirations, fears, anticipations, and other states of minds directed toward the future. If I have grouped all this under the head of fantasies, it is because imagination plays so great a role here. We are afraid of what may happen, not of what will happen, for we do not know what will happen. Yet whatever plans we make for tomorrow must be laid upon the probable. We hope that tomorrow will be a continuation of today, that the paper will be left at the door, that the telephone lines will be working, that the trains will be running, that the electricity will operate as usual, and most of the time our hopes are justified. But there are, after all, disasters and strikes and accidental interruptions to the continuity of history. Yet if we did not establish a routine upon which we could count, the daily conduct of life would be impossible.

Our concerns for the future run between the two extremes of rational planning and day-dreaming. Both emerge out of and are in some way conditioned by the past. Consequently, what has been strained out of our past life remains in our memory to direct the anticipation of the future. It may seem strange to include what has not been realized in our inventory of experience. But our wishes, though not as yet fulfilled, are present now. And being present, they may decide what we shall see and hear now, as well as what we shall do tomorrow.

As a matter of fact some of the most powerful incentives to action have been ideas of the future. Of these everyone knows about the idea of progress which made life happier for thousands at the beginning of the present century. Another was the idea known as millenarianism, according to which at some date in the future, previously thought to be the year 1000, Christ would descend to earth and the Day of Judgment would be at hand. The American idea of Manifest Destiny concerned the future of the United States. And the well-known verse of Bishop Berkeley, "Westward the course of empire takes its way," laid out a plan for the political future of the world. In fact, what is prophecy but a fantasy of the future even if inspired? And the Greeks seldom made a move without consulting the oracle at Delphi about its probable outcome.

5. *The inner life.* Another item that certainly belongs to experience as one of its foci is what is referred to as our "inner life." I am using this term to cover our estimate of ourselves, our self-satisfaction and self-dissatisfaction, our hostility to ourselves and our self-love or self-

gratification. We are aware at times that we have not behaved as well as we might have, and we either feel ashamed of ourselves or justified. We either blame ourselves for what we have done or excuse ourselves. We have phrases like, "I don't see what else I could have done under the circumstances"; "I just stood up and told him what I thought"; "I was proud of my upbringing"; "What would you have done in my place?" All such phrases are focused on one's self and there have been psychologists who have declared that the self is always present in all experience. It is said to be the center, that which "has" the experience, the agent which is conscious. If this is true, then certainly one of the foci of experience is the self or that which corresponds to the first personal pronoun.

This classification of mine is admittedly rough and might be simplified by an analytical psychologist. But the differences indicated exist on the level on which we are operating. I shall now try to suggest how these foci may influence the occurrence of new ideas.

First, we wake up in the morning and we hear a bird which we think we have never heard before. We look out the window and we see that the willows are beginning to turn yellow. We shave and find that the razor blade is tugging at our beard. We go to the bus or train or to the garage for the car and find the first may be unusually late or that the battery of the car is dead. Before dinner we sit down to drink a martini and find that the vermouth is used up. There is surely no need to illustrate my point any further. In all these and similar cases we become aware that something new has happened. The routine has been interrupted. Our habits have been broken. It is like hearing a false note on the piano or stumbling on the stairs. It may well be this rupture of habit that makes us aware of novelty.

But it also stimulates our curiosity by first calling our attention to the fact of novelty and by second raising the question of why. If problems are defined as perceived deviations from the rule, then obviously as soon as we have spotted such a deviation, we have been confronted with a problem. The question now is how to explain it. Old generalizations may no longer work. But explanation always consists in absorbing the problematic into an accepted class of things and events. We assume that the larger classes must have formal regularity—that is an assumption of method. But over the centuries various types of formal regularity have been sought. Sometimes it has been assumed that all change is purposive and the scientist looked for the aim or goal or end of every change. A subtype of universal purpose has been human purpose—all change is for the good of the human race. Hence when one man would say that the universal purpose was God's purpose which might, but need not, be beyond human understanding, another would say that all purpose could best be thought of as human welfare, a doctrine that might be called cosmic benevolence or philanthropy. The first man would say, for instance, that rain fell to the earth to keep up the perfect balance of the four elements (earth, water, air, and fire); the second, that it fell to make the crops grow.

At other times explanation has been purely causal, according to which something, called the cause, precedes the change in question and generates the change. This type of explanation too had several forms. One form maintained that anything whatever which always preceded the change was the cause of the change: the will of the gods or other ambient spirits, human desires, the position of the planets, or, on a less dramatic plane, blows and collisions of material particles. But since this was a kind of explanation which could not be controlled, was often incapable of verification, and had little practical value, its partisans refined it as the years went on until only regular series of material events became acceptable as causes. Even psychological events were attributed to material causes, the nervous system usually.

Suppose a man believed that rain was caused by the Raingod. How would he behave? There are naturally several possibilities. He might be the resigned type who takes what he gets and is glad to get it even if disagreeable. If it rains enough to help the crops he may be thankful and express his thanks by appropriate rites. If there is a drought, he shrugs his shoulders in resignation or makes a sacrifice which custom tells him will please the Raingod and perhaps induce him to break the drought. If, however, he is a more aggressive type, he may curse out the Raingod, threaten to cut off all dances and sacrifices, or look elsewhere for water because the Raingod is unreliable. In short, there is no proof that the failure of an idea will lead to invention or improvisation or even to a change of mind. But there is good reason to believe that unless an idea proves false or unworkable, it will never be dropped. This inertia of custom bestows an air of inevitability on any idea, an air of rightness which has a compulsive force over those who have been accepting it. There are habits of belief as well as habits of action and the former are as compulsive as the latter. One can have a sense of guilt from breaking the most insignificant habits or customs. The morning papers carry columns of letters to this or that authority who makes a business of giving the traditional answers on what to do or not do on all occasions from birth to death.

The affective coefficients of an idea are more influential than the failure of an idea to work. The idea that a Raingod makes it rain might be very pleasant; for gods, when they are friendly, are enough like human beings to be loved and, when they are unfriendly, to be feared. Gods made in the image of men are also comprehensible. They are not nebulous metaphysical principles but beings who act more or less as humans do. Usually they are more consistent than human beings, for they have a fairly narrow range of function. One would not expect Vulcan to help in agriculture or Venus to be of much use in medicine. In this way they resemble patron saints who specialize in helping jewelers, carpenters, washerwomen, and sailors. You would not pray to St. Eloi if you were a cobbler; you would pray to St. Crispin. Motorists seek the protection of St. Christopher and mariners that of St. Anne. Some find lost objects; others help students pass examinations; some even help in childbirth. This must be a delightful belief, and since one can always explain away a god's indifference—"My prayer was faulty in wording or perhaps insincere"; "My sacrifice was not properly performed"; "I was unworthy"—one clings to the belief.

If, however, the same belief is unpleasant, then one may try to replace it with another which is more agreeable. Some people might find it very disagreeable to believe that the earth, the waters upon it, the air over our heads, and the stars in heaven were all peopled with these divinities. Varro is said to have counted 40,000 of them —invisible yet powerful, interfering in human affairs, spying on one, unreliable in their favors. In this case a man might decide to test the whole idea. He might test it in a variety of ways, by observing whether he might omit his prayers, dances, sacrifices, and not be punished by the neglected god. This would require unusual courage. He might discuss the matter with his contemporaries, who would probably be adolescents, and at least express doubts. He might simply admit to himself that he felt uncomfortable in the constant presence of these deities and thus be receptive to a new idea. The problem then would be how to rid himself of this intellectual discomfort. I suspect that no one by his own unaided efforts ever framed a new idea. But once one has admitted to oneself one's dissatisfaction with customary ideas, the way is open to conversion.

It should be said at this point that since human beings live in societies, there are always going to be meetings with others who disagree. I have no doubt that for every argument that could be advanced against the existence of Raingods, another could be framed to oppose it. For the very existence of divinities presupposes conditions that are antithetical to natural conditions. All proofs and disproofs of existence are based upon tests, not argument, and these tests by their very nature are prior to any dialectical proofs. A divinity need not be visible, tactual, or otherwise perceptible. And whereas we might disprove the existence of an absolutely imperceptible apple, we could not disprove the existence of an absolutely imperceptible god. Hence social intercourse might weaken our faith in our divinities, but it would not do so by the logic of conviction. It would utilize the logic of persuasion. And that logic addresses itself to the feelings. By making an idea unpleasant, repulsive, ridiculous, disturbing, one makes it more or less unacceptable, and the person who is being influenced is prepared to change his mind. In saying this I am simply asserting that ideas have an affective charge which may be counted on to play a role in debate.

Memory enters at this point, and the past either corrects or reinforces the present. Since history must record both the duration of an idea and its mutations, it should be noted that sometimes an idea is retained even if it is not supported by the past or the present. Again we resort to the inertia of custom, which strengthens beliefs that have been held for a long period of time. Sometimes, however, the words in which a belief is expressed are retained while the belief itself is modified and other times the words are changed and the belief retained. As an example of the former, we have the idea of popular sovereignty, which in Rome probably meant the sovereignty of the Patricians until the revolt of the Plebeians in 494 B.C. This revolt led to the establishment of the Tribunate of the Plebs, after which the Plebeians were given more and more power. The term "the People" was used throughout the Middle Ages, as it was in Rome and as it is used today, but the idea which it names has changed constantly. (We discuss this below in Chapter 8.) As an example of retaining old beliefs under new names, the most interesting example is the retention of pagan ceremonies under Christian names, the Saturnalia with the *libertas Decembri* turning into Christmas and Easter becoming the Festival of the Resurrection. Similarly Apollo turns into St. Sebastian and Hercules into St. Christopher, as far as their looks are concerned.

It would seem as if ideas would not change of their own accord, and that there is as much resistance to changing one's ideas, whether of fact or of value, as there is to changing one's character. Yet to live in an intellectual milieu—like a college—which does not fortify the ideas one had carried over from childhood, may shock one into abandoning one's memories and confronting a new set of thoughts. The unrest on the part of the present undergraduate population is perhaps due to their hearing the same things at college as they heard at home, and consequently they feel none of that effervescence which an earlier generation experienced in the presence of something novel. To some, the meeting of new ideas head-on is traumatic, and to all it must prove bewildering. If it is not disastrous, the new intellectual environment provides a stimulus to forming new ideas. Why some individuals react favorably to this is not known. We say that such people have open minds, but that is simply a name for the fact that they do react favorably. Probably one of the strongest factors making for such receptivity is one's admiration for the people who hold an idea rather than for the idea itself. It is certainly not the evidence pro and con which changes one's attitude toward an idea. For the man who is faced with the problem of changing his mind has not enough information at his disposal upon which to base a rational judgment. If he had, he would already be on the road to conversion. Moreover it is part of traditional wisdom to let well enough alone. But if an undergraduate takes a course under an instructor whom, for reasons of which he is unaware, he admires, it is likely that he will transfer his admiration for the man to the man's ideas.

This is well illustrated in political and religious orations and to almost the same degree in aesthetic criticism. The oratorical technique of the politician relies on painting a rosy picture of what life will be like under his rule, but seldom goes into the technical problems of finances, of finding adequately trained people to realize his dreams, of disposing of the dead wood of the bureaucracy, of frustrating greed and the lust for power. The orator is a lyric poet singing of his yearning for the good, his love for his audience, his contempt for his opponents. In the 1956 presidential elections Adlai Stevenson gave four speeches outlining the plans he would try to carry out if elected. These speeches were almost unique in American history in their detail. But the public press was of the opinion that the candidate was above the heads of the public. It is much more effective to tell the voters what your goal is, not how you are going to reach it.

Sermons are similar in that they create a state of mind which is assumed to be the preliminary to moral and religious reform. They hope to make their hearers penitent, hopeful, fearful, or ecstatic. They need not be argumentative. In the preface to *The Genius of Christianity* Chateaubriand, who had been a skeptic in his youth, wrote that when he heard of his mother's death, he wept and he believed. William James in his *Varieties of Religious Experience* gives other examples of conversions induced by nonlogical means. For our purposes it is enough to know that resistance to new ideas might be reduced by the removal of emotional obstacles to their acceptance. It is assumed that there will always be obstacles of some sort.

Similar comments may be made about our fantasies of the future. One might imagine that if one has a dream of a better state of affairs, the next step would be to plan for its realization. But in nine cases out of ten the next step is to talk about it. Someone else less given to dreaming and more to acting is pleased with the idea and proceeds to work out plans for making it real. Thus two or more people often make the same invention at about the same time. Invention is a social affair, however unsocial inventors may be, and depends on the reading and study and conversations of dozens of people before it comes to fruition. Nor should it be forgotten that no matter how grateful later generations are to inventors, few if any inventions when proposed have been given a cordial reception. In the field of belief an invention is a heresy; in the field of self-interest it is a prospective financial disaster.

Finally, an individual may get a new idea as he tries to integrate his inner conflicts, to subdue his hostility to others (as well as to himself). He learns to make a new estimate not only of his own life but of living in general. Usually this is accomplished under the guidance of a psychiatrist, clergyman, or friend. It would be almost impossible in isolation. For one of the most startling new ideas is that one is neither perfect in the eyes of others nor omnipotent. One's imperfections are pointed out by critics whose attitude may range from extreme hostility to fraternal counsel. One's limited powers need no reporter. But in both cases resignation may result rather than reform and the new ideas be shrugged off. One can always say that one cares nothing for the opinions of others, just as one can withdraw into an environment which is more manipulable. The Big Man in a small village is bound to have the illusion of great potency.

How Ideas Change

The most general sources of new ideas may be listed as follows.

Inference. This is best illustrated in the history of philosophy and of the sciences. When it seemed to be established by Descartes that the mind and the body were two entirely distinct substances, it was inferred that they could not interact. But in volition it looked as if the mind caused motion in the body, and in sensation it looked as if the body caused effects in the mind. It was inferred by Malebranche and those philosophers called Occasionalists that at such moments God brought about the result as by a sort of miracle, and it was held by Spinoza that the apparent interaction did not and could not take place. Hence Spinoza concluded that every event was both mental and physical, depending on the point of view from which it was studied. Again, when Lamarck observed that by using certain muscles we increase their size, that by exercising our hands in various ways we increase their agility, he inferred that it was possible by use and disuse to change to some degree bodily structure. By assuming that such changes could be inherited, as musical talent seems to be hereditary, he inferred that higher organisms could have developed from lower. The giraffe got his long neck from his ancestors' having persistently reached for the upper and tenderer shoots of trees.

Random association. How scientists get a new idea is somewhat of a mystery and it has been said that much of their work is done while they are sleeping. Hamilton's discovery of quaternions came to him as he was walking with his wife. She was talking to him about ordinary subjects and he suddenly got the great idea. What suggested the idea to him is no longer discoverable but the point is that it just popped into his mind. Wallace Stevens wrote a poem called "Celle Qui Fut Héaulmiette." This was inspired by seeing Rodin's statue usually called "The Old Courtesan" but which was in turn inspired by Villon's poem, "La Belle Héaulmière." In view of the fact that analogy plays so large a part in rudimentary science, it is understandable that random association should suggest analogies which may later turn out to trigger the rise of a new idea.

Active curiosity. There is no discounting the role of curiosity. A person wants to know what would happen *if* . . . One imagines Lewis Carroll, who was a mathematician, saying to himself, "What would happen in a world in which everything was reversed as in a mirror?" And *Through the Looking Glass* was the result. Horticulture furnishes dozens of examples of results attained by crossing varieties which had not been previously crossed. Kepler's final discovery of the elliptical shape of the planetary orbits is a classic example of what dogged curiosity will achieve.

Other people. The influence of other people, not only as given in conversation and teaching but also in books, cannot be underestimated. Philosophers, scientists, novelists, and poets depend for their sustenance on the ideas of others. All writers almost without exception can be grouped in schools, tendencies, intellectual or aesthetic groups, and it is fair to say that no man thinks in solitude. Moreover, none of the sources mentioned here operates alone and they are sorted out by me in a manner which might well be criticized as exaggeration. An empty mind will never be filled.

In all four situations the man who gets the new idea must assume that some new ideas are both true and valuable. The instinctive intellectual Tory will deny this; the instinctive intellectual Whig will substitute "all" for "some" and insist that a new idea is worth entertaining because it is new. The philosopher will weigh each idea as it comes. There are very few philosophers.

So far we can conclude that to understand why ideas have a history requires a broad definition of "experience." What I have called the foci of experience could just as well be called the facets of experience. It is important to observe that all are interrelated in spite of their different names and the possibility of talking about them separately. So one can talk about the brain without talking about the blood, but the brain will be inoperative without a steady blood supply, and the blood supply comes from the heart and has to be oxygenated by the lungs— and all this depends upon food in the long run. Ideas of course may originate in perceptual material but are classified and organized in view of our interests modified by how we feel about them. Since no two people's experiences are exactly alike, no two people will entirely agree except for social purposes. These purposes include the conventional use of language, peaceful coexistence in schools, and successful adjustment to the various social groups to which one belongs.

It should not be forgotten, however, that some ideas are the possessions of groups of men and not merely of individuals. We shall next take up the question of why ideas change.

·4·

Ideas and Social History

Ideas both of fact and of policy may be held by groups as well as by individuals and they may also be protected by groups. In fact, the common belief in certain ideas determines the nature of the group which believes in it. In 1968 there were in the United States about 961 societies, exclusive of religious sects, organized for or against something: adult education, aeronautics, agronomy (at the beginning of the alphabet) and republicanism, Youth Hostelry, and Zionism (at the end). Clearly if you subscribe to or work for the Humane Society, it is because you believe in its program and will think it worth money and time to protect animals from man's cruelty. And if you are a member of a temperance society, you believe that drinking is bad. Whether you will apply the program of the society in your daily life—being kind to animals and

abstaining from alcohol—is another matter. We are talking about ideas, not about behavior.

Your commitment to the program of a given society
does not entail your commitment to all the other ideas
that its various members may support. You can be a
sincere member of the Planned Parenthood Association
and not a member of the W.C.T.U., the U.N. Association, or the D.A.R. This should be obvious but it is sometimes overlooked. You can be to the Left on some issues
and to the Right on others. But in a country where
clubs, societies, and professional associations are so
numerous, you are bound to be allied with people for one
cause with whom you would be in disagreement on
others. A Daughter of the American Revolution would
not necessarily be an admirer of Gounod; she might even
prefer Schönberg. I emphasize this because, though it
is true that ideas are determined in part by their social
correlatives, people do not live in all of society but in
limited social groups.

The prestige of some of these organizations extends to
their programs, and people will tend to accept the program of a group whose prestige is high. It is noticeable
that many of them have lists of sponsors on their
stationery; the sponsors are there not to work for the
organization or because they know a great deal about
the necessity of its program, but because their names
are well known to the public which will be asked for
contributions. Sometimes, in fact, the lists are laughable.
Actors, singers, novelists, athletes, couturiers will appear

as sponsors for an organization urging the control of some disease. They would be the last people on earth to pretend to know anything of a technical nature about the disease in question but, since they are kindhearted and hate the idea of people getting sick, they "lend their names" to a campaign to eliminate sickness.

None of this has any logical connection with the idea that is being propagated. But it is an illustration of how an idea can be propagated. It is always easier to agree that an evil should be eliminated than to agree on the technique for doing it. Almost everyone is agreed that cancer, international warfare, murder, and ignorance should be done away with. The exceptions are those men who believe that all evils are divine punishments for human sins. But the slightest acquaintance with discussions on how to do away with cancer or war or any other evil will show that bitter arguments arise over whether teams of doctors or individuals working alone are the more efficacious; whether disarmament or arbitration is better; whether stronger punishment or psychiatry would be the better deterrent to crime; whether more public libraries or planned adult education would be the more illuminating. The professional soldier and the pacifist will agree that war is an evil, but one will preach preparedness and the other nonviolence. The Christian Scientist and the doctor will agree that cancer ought to be eliminated, but from that point on they part company. So with the other issues.

The groups formed for the promotion of certain ideas are themselves operating within a much larger collection known as Society with an initial capital. Society in this sense has a program which, at a minimum, consists of (a) self-perpetuation, (b) the preservation of certain traditions or in a general sense the status quo, and (c) the passing of statutes. The only societies that have ever committed suicide are one or two so-called primitive tribes confronted by the challenge of Occidental civilization. The Jews of York committed suicide as a body during the massacres of the twelfth century. Some groups have fought against their aggressors to the death, but that is self-defense; and one of the cardinal principles of every Society is the right to self-defense. Hence when a modern state wishes to make war on another, it immediately announces that it is doing so because it is threatened from without. In 1941 the Rhine was said to be the American frontier. In 1964 the frontier moved to the Gulf of Tonkin.[1] The Soviet Union has acted in a similar fashion and is the Victim of Aggression even when, as in Hungary, a local rebellion is going on or when, as in Czechoslovakia, it disapproves of the regime. Both states when engaged in such adventures are talking

[1] Feb. 12, 1955, the U.S. agreed to train the South Vietnamese army.

Oct. 22, 1957, the first injuries to U.S. advisers were reported.

July 8, 1959, first U.S. troops killed.

Dec. 1962, the U.S. force is 4,000.

Dec. 1963, the U.S. force is 15,000.

Aug. 7, 1964, Tonkin Gulf Resolution.

Dec. 1964, U.S. force is 23,000.

Nov. 1966, U.S. force is 358,000.

Figures from the *World Almanac*, 1968.

ideological language, the United States blocking the Communist Menace, the U.S.S.R. blocking the inroads of Bourgeois Capitalist Imperialism. Neither country has had its land invaded since 1945, but both have substituted ideological frontiers for geographic.

Thus both countries seem to maintain that they stand for a tradition, in this case an economic tradition. Since the beginning of the New Economic Policy the Soviet Union has softened the rigidity of orthodox Marxism and the United States has never permitted orthodox free enterprise since it inaugurated protective tariffs in 1789. In the Soviet Union the state owns the tools of production; in the United States the state controls and supervises their use, invoking usually the interstate commerce clause in self-justification. Both systems are hard to define clearly, but the two names "Communism" and "Free Enterprise" serve very well as slogans and only a handful of people in either country worry about the precise meaning of the slogans. The economic traditions are not the only traditions that distinguish the two states, but they are the two which seem to be the most important, an ironic tribute to Karl Marx.

Statutes, our third constituent element of a Society, are like traditions since observance of them—or disregard of them—becomes customary. Many of these statutes are similar to those in the books of Leviticus and Deuteronomy. Statutes regulating sexual relations and marriage, for instance, may resemble Anglo-Saxon customs but they were framed in accordance with biblical injunctions and were sanctioned by the Church. Many of the statutes of Massachusetts date from the days when the colonists thought that they were living in a theocracy and the only theocratic laws they had ever heard of were in the Old Testament. Many statutes have remained on the books though they are seldom observed. In the United States, for instance, there are laws against polygamy. But most men are polygamous in practice though not in theory and are protected by the law from performing all the duties of a husband to their mistresses or concubines.

Now such statutes plus the prohibitions of the Ten Commandments are so interwoven into the fabric of Occidental societies that we require a strong initiation before violating them. Swearing begins fairly soon, Sabbath-breaking a bit later, adultery after adolescence, though fornication comes earlier; theft begins in childhood but is abandoned by most adults; murder is unusual; perjury is perhaps abhorred by all and only practiced by advice of counsel when it is likely to be an evasion of the truth rather than out-and-out lying. But the infractions of the Decalogue, like the Seven Deadly Sins, are recognized as evils even by the people who commit them. For we are all educated from childhood to regard these laws as divinely revealed. They form a nucleus of ideas that we have accepted—that we have been obliged to accept—before we realize that there is any alternative to them. Our parents, our siblings, the school, the Church, as well as the state, drum them into us so that when we begin to lie or swear we have an easily recognized twinge of conscience.

It is a metaphor, but a legitimate one, to call them the anatomy of our Society. They give an ideological structure to our Society and when violations of them occur on a noticeable scale, we feel that the very existence of our culture is threatened. The skeleton of such standards is a combination of the rights to live and to own property, wives being included under property, and both are protected by the emphasis that is placed on telling the truth under oath. The idea that the oath will ensure veracity, however, rests on the assumption that the juror believes in God. But men and women who have been married "in the sight of God and this company" have nevertheless broken their marriage vows. It has been possible in the United States for people who object to oaths to "affirm," and it is obvious that men have perjured themselves to gain ends which they believe to be more important than telling the truth. So men have violated all the laws both statutory and common, and in the United States they are doing so in increasing percentages. Murder, for instance, has increased by an average of 22 per cent in 1967, running from 13 per cent in the South to 36 per cent in the North Central states. Forcible rape has increased by an average of 7.3 per cent, and here the South ranks highest with an increase of 11 per cent and the North Central states with an increase of only 4 per cent. These differences can be explained and the explanation is not merely an ideological matter. But clearly a murderer has not learned to discipline his aggressions and, were he able to stop and think before committing murder, he would have to admit that the life of his proposed victim could be spared without loss.

There is therefore a margin of tolerance between the anatomy and the physiology of a Society as I have been describing it. Just as a diseased human body may have the same organs as a well one but nevertheless function badly, so our Society has all the organs of one in good health but they are not in working order. Unfortunately we have no social physicians and surgeons to remedy matters and here my metaphor, like most analogies, breaks down. We act as if our behavior could be made to conform to our ideas, an assumption that has been in vogue ever since Plato and Aristotle. But there is also the possibility that our ideas are a reflection of human behavior. And when they are codified in the form of statute, they reflect only the behavior of the date of codification. People of the twentieth century simply cannot be expected to hold life dear. Their governments have thrown it away on the fields of battle and also, let it not be forgotten, in the horrors of our urban slums, which are worldwide, and in the villages surrounding factories in time of war. I am not the first to point out that the distinction between combatant and noncombatant has disappeared; anyone who saw the ruins of England and France and Germany in 1945 knows that it is laughable to talk about sparing the lives of civilians. Since custom is always stronger than statute, our increase in felonies may be the reflection of the increase in slaughter as ordained on a wholesale scale by the state.

What I have said, if true, would simply emphasize what most of us know, that there are two sets of ideas in every Society. First there are those which are embodied in the laws and second those which are embedded in practice. The second are found in literature and in conversation, in novels, plays, poems, both literal and allegorical. Satire again is a frequent source of information on what people think they should do as against what the laws of God and the state prescribe. To call patterns of behavior ideas is to stretch the denotation of the term, for they are not formulated into ideas by the men who most clearly exhibit them. A rake does not usually have a conscious philosophy of debauchery. When his sins are pointed out, he will excuse himself in one or more of the well-known manners of apology. It is very doubtful whether a habitual thief would not object to being robbed. It is more likely that such violators of the moral taboos would flatly deny that they had violated them. Few hypocrites admit their hypocrisy, few liars their mendacity. And there are probably only selected occasions—such as that presented by the confessional—on which they would admit their errors. But there are also probably only certain occasions on which they would be hypocritical or mendacious—those when their self-esteem is endangered.

The conflict between the way in which people behave and the way they "ought" to behave concerns the historian of ideas in two ways, mainly when the conflict stimulates the formation of new ideas of what ought to be and, secondarily, when attempts are made to determine the ruling ideas of a period.

There are times, such as the early Christian centuries,

the late sixteenth century, the 1960's, when large numbers of people reject authority, live in accordance with new standards, and above all justify their behavior in speeches and essays. There have always been recalcitrant people, but I am speaking of times when their numbers are impressive enough to induce the authorities to take notice. In the early Christian period the authorities resorted to persecution; in the sixteenth century they resorted to the stake; but in the 1960's they have practiced *laisser-faire* and compromise. In the first two periods mentioned, the authorities finally yielded. By the fourth century (A.D. 313) Christianity had become the state religion. By 1545 the Counter Reformation had begun with the opening of the Council of Trent. The revolts of the 1960's are revolts against war, poverty, racial discrimination, ignorance, and even social etiquette, and on the whole authority has been lenient compared to the precedents it might have followed. The one exception to this leniency has been protests against the war in Vietnam. This exception is significant, since the state enforces its foreign policy by its armed forces and that policy, as we have said above, is expressed as self-defense. In this case it is an economic program, Marxism, which we have been fighting, a program which we feel threatens the existence of our own program, so that our war is an extension of our economic philosophy. The fundamental question is the antecedent of the pronoun "our."

When Christianity and Protestantism won their battles, there immediately developed new conflicts within each group, the various Christian heresies continued to harass the authorities after the Edict of Milan (A.D. 313) and there developed various sects of Protestantism after Luther's victory. There are now over two hundred Protestant sects in the United States alone. Thus the unity during a struggle against something becomes disunity once the struggle is successful.[2] The Edict of Milan, besides everything else, was an edict of tolerance. The idea of tolerance, which was called indifference by the youthful Lamennais, assumes that what is being tolerated is as true, as right, as reasonable as the ideas that it has been opposing. To tolerate such ideas is to act as if everyone had a right to believe in anything, however absurd. To a Roman pagan the Edict of Milan seemed to be saying that the ideas emanating from an obscure—and detested—tribe in Asia Minor were as sound as the ideas that had grown up on Italian soil some centuries before, consecrated by the Senate and the People, applied by the augurs and priests, and proved to be true by the victories of the Republic and Empire. It did not do this in so many words. It permitted people to be Christians without danger of persecution. And it was followed in time by making Christianity the official religion of the Empire. Our pagan, reading the Edict, would have argued that Constantine must believe that there could be two antithetical truths about the same subject matter—and this is nonsense if religious ideas are

[2] The initial unity lay in what the Reformers were against, not in what they were for. This may explain the present diversity.

ideas of fact. It just is not true that the earth is flat, and though we would no longer punish a man if he believed it to be flat, we would not appoint him a professor of geography either. If, on the other hand, there is no evidence one way or the other, we are likely to say that a man can believe whatever he chooses. No one is going to argue about who succeeded King Oberon or what was the color of Pegasus.

Subjects about which there is no evidence are usually, but not always, fantasies. Like the song the Sirens sang, they are not beyond conjecture, but can be answered only by conjecture. If religious ideas are of that nature, then freedom of conscience is indeed an inalienable right. To be tolerant about them amounts to granting that they —or some of them—are neither true nor false, or that they may suggest beautiful or repugnant pictures, or that they are like a piece of music, incitements to dreams. Few religious people would take such a position. On the contrary, like the Ultramontanists, they would say that there can be no doubt about such dogmas, that they are absolutely true, rooted in divine revelation as found both in Scripture and in tradition. The Laodicean posture will not do.

Our third example, drawn from contemporary life, shows an even broader extent of tolerance. For now it covers not merely matters of fact but matters of policy as well. Such policies as the limitation of births was first recorded in Genesis 38:9, and it was condemned by the authorities and Onan was killed. This tradition has been perpetuated by the Roman Catholic Church. At the same time, people everywhere who did not want children practiced some form of contraception and did not worry whether it was approved by the Church or not. A generation ago birth-control clinics were established for the use of special cases. Now birth control is governmental policy in some countries and information about contraception is available to all. Indeed some people have argued for obligatory sterilization for men and women whom they believe to be unfit to have children. This is a dramatic reversal of ideas and even within the Church of Rome, where continence was first preached, profiting from the periodicity of ovulation took its place. That is as far as the Church has been willing to go to date.

If one ask how this reversal has come about, the most satisfactory answer is man's confrontation with overpopulation. If there is not going to be enough food to feed the children that are born, what is the sense in bearing them? There clearly is no sense and the birth rate ought to decline. The Catholic Church has never denied this conclusion, as far as I know, but has maintained that the most moral way not to have children is by being continent for thus one avoids the taking of life. The extension of tolerance was manifested when people began to say in effect, "We shall not be continent and we shall not have children either." At this point the idea that copulation was for the exclusive purpose of having children, as ordained by the Creator, was flatly denied. It was held to be self-justified. It was undeniably man's most intense pleasure and such a pleasure should not be condemned. Are we to condemn eating because it leads to gluttony? trade because it leads to cheating and avarice? clothing because it leads to extravagance and ostentation? The analogies are a bit lame, but it was indisputable that sexual pleasure was not to be eliminated. Men had known ever since the sixteenth century that promiscuity led to the spread of venereal disease. The remedy sought was not sexual discipline but prevention and therapy. Out of this emerges one suggested conclusion: when the desire to violate a law, whether religious, moral, or civic, is strong, the law will be violated and the violation justified. The Sixth Commandment has never been applied to warfare, nor to the extirpation of heresy.

The relation between the idea that the world is over-populated and the idea that conception should be controlled may sound logical but it is really pragmatic. Strictly speaking, it would seem that the way not to have children is to be chaste. But this is not practical. By that we mean that most people would prefer not to be chaste. To gratify our sexual appetites and at the same time not have children is reinterpreted to mean the gratification of the appetite plus control of the size of the population. Put in this way the hedonistic factor is preserved and the practical result obtained. Along with the practical result has been the increase of sexual pleasure among adolescents and the spread of venereal disease among them too. The hedonistic argument has operated in isolation from the foreseeable effects of its acceptance. Some adolescents seem willing to risk both venereal disease and pregnancy.

We observe here how the supposed need of Society may modify ideas. Whatever may have been the case in primitive times, modern society has developed publicly supported institutions to protect the intellectual, moral, physical, aesthetic, and economic welfare of its members. Some people have objected to some features of this, but most of it is so built into the modern state that to eradicate it would result in chaos. If it were to be proposed that the states abandon the practice of licensing physicians, the public would be horrified. Public health is a concern of the state and must be supervised by the state! But the Department of Health, Education and Welfare was established in the United States only in 1953. As a matter of interest to the historian of ideas, we list the dates on which the various cabinet offices were instituted. The list indicates when certain ideas were first thought to deserve social protection and how the federal government assumed more and more responsibilities. Thus George Washington had three members in his cabinet: the secretaries of State, War, and Treasury. The office of Postmaster-General was part of the Treasury and the Attorney-General was not made a member of the cabinet until 1814. To all intents and purposes it is fair to say that foreign relations, public monies, war, communication, and justice were believed to be matters of federal interest almost at the beginning of the republic. The organization of the Navy Department dates from 1798;

of the Interior from 1849; of Agriculture from 1862; of Commerce and Labor from 1903 to be split in two ten years later; of Health, Education and Welfare from 1953; of Housing and Urban Development from 1965; and of Transportation from 1966. It would be absurd to maintain that this is a history only of ideas; it marks real changes in institutions. But the fact that Congress was willing to authorize these new offices as time went on leads one to conclude that its ideas about governmental responsibilities had grown. They had grown from ideas about protection from external enemies and finances to protection from those internal enemies which are inherent in an urban civilization.

Such ideas are properly called the ideas of Society at large, even though minority groups disapprove of them. For they have been espoused by those persons who have been elected by the majority of voters to represent them and, theoretically, to speak in their name. These ideas have been embodied in institutions which are recognized as part of the Executive branch of the government and are supported by grants from Congress. Yet, like all ideas, they are subject to debate and with the passage of years even the oldest of them have been modified. Foreign affairs are not carried on today as they were in Washington's day and foreign policy has been profoundly changed. To take but two instances of this, American foreign policy was isolationist until 1918, though the erosion of isolationism started with the pronouncement of the Monroe Doctrine. In the second place, few if any persons thought it was the duty of the United States to guarantee by force of arms the constitution of any other state. The policy was that of noninterference in the internal affairs of another country. But just as isolationism was rejected when we annexed Hawaii, so noninterference was rejected when we intervened in South Vietnam. Old institutions are diverted from their original aims to suit the needs of the moment. But those needs have to be voiced by someone, Esau or Jacob.

In studying the history of ideas, it is essential to distinguish those which are incorporated in institutions, and therefore change slowly, from those which are the opinions of individual persons and are transmitted from man to man, and change more rapidly. One can see both rates of change in politics and religion, on the one hand, and in science and philosophy, on the other. Such political principles as national sovereignty or such religious principles as divine justice have barely been altered since people began writing about them. But the ideas that individuals have expressed about these principles, when they have been free to express them, have varied greatly. There is no church in the Occident that denies God's eternal justice and no state which limits its autonomy. Where the former seems dubitable, the doubter is silenced by the retort that the Will of God is inscrutable. Where the latter is obviously limited by treaty, it is pointed out that the treaty was freely made and approved by the Senate.

Science and philosophy are in a quite different situation. Though both scientists and philosophers have pupils and work in groups, the history of each shows a high degree of independence not only in the conclusions reached but also in the methods of reaching them. Physics, chemistry, and biology today are basically different from the sciences out of which they emerged. No one a few generations ago used the statistical method in any of these fields. The theory of probability formerly was held to be a substitute for human ignorance. Now it is used as a matter of course in all three fields. At the beginning of the twentieth century a chemical element was believed to be unchangeable; now elements are born in laboratories. At the same time psychologists were using the method of introspection as standard procedure and many of them were analyzing "mental states" into their elementary sensations; now some form of behaviorism has taken the place of introspection and it is doubtful whether anyone believes in elementary sensations. Philosophy has undergone as many mutations as science, and whereas the American undergraduate of sixty years ago would have identified philosophy with English Neo-Hegelianism, today he identifies it with linguistic analysis.

All this suggests that when an idea is adopted by a group and put into practice, as in a church or a state, its rate of change will be slow. When, on the contrary, it is the property of an individual who is free to "change his mind," his mind will probably change. For there is such a thing as learning from experience, and as a man grows older, his experience usually widens. Since the world is not all of a piece but enters our lives in various forms, the only way for our minds not to change is for our environment to remain stable. One can live in ignorance of everything beyond one's front door. Everything outside that barrier may be distorted by legend and superstition. And yet life will continue its humdrum course and one will be untroubled by curiosity. This would be the life of the peasant on his acre of ground. The cultural primitivist would admire the simplicity of such a life. On the other hand, as soon as one walks down the village street, one is struck by new sights and new voices, and at that moment the danger of changing one's mind arises. Since the twentieth century with its world wars, radio, television, and aeronautics has made "travel" inevitable even if one stays at home, ideas change like the patterns in a kaleidoscope. That ideas could have a history may have been thought of before the twentieth century, but that their history was worth studying is a very modern suggestion.

· 5 ·

Systems of Ideas

It has been customary to think of ideas as organized into systems which have a kind of internal unity. The unity in question arises out of a desire on the part of a thinker to be logically consistent. Logical consistency in a system is best illustrated by plane geometry where all the theorems and their consequences can be traced back to the definitions, axioms, and postulates which are stated at the outset of Book I. In natural science and philosophy such formal rigor is impossible. The scientist prefers to check his inferences by experiment, and the philosopher who wishes to go beyond the data of perception has to indulge in speculation. But he will try to keep his speculations rational. Behind both kinds of thinking lies the assumption that the universe is intelligible in that it is possible to find a set of logically related propositions that will describe it. This is an assumption because no one really knows to what extent it is true. It is a rule of procedure and a good one, for without it any fantasy would be acceptable as scientific.

Sometimes it is said that there is another type of unity which the philosopher must seek, organic unity. Organic unity is metaphorical. It is the unity that living organisms are said to have. An animal is believed to behave as a whole that is not simply the arithmetical sum of its parts. There is no logical connection between respiration and the circulation of the blood. In fact Harvey himself did not notice that there was any physiological connection. Yet the oxygen of the air is taken in by the lungs, and the blood which is pumped out of the heart gets oxygenated in the lungs. It flows back to the heart through the veins and thus forms a closed circuit. Without blood the brain would not function; hence the brain is functionally dependent upon both the heart and the lungs. One could continue in this way and demonstrate the body's unity in a primary-school manner. It is clearly the unity of interdependence.

A system of ideas may have organic unity in the sense that even if its "parts" do not logically emanate from one or two propositions, they are all necessary to construct the system. The parts in question are those propositions and their interrelations which comprise the system under examination. I shall try to give two examples of ideological systems. The first will be from philosophy, Schopenhauer's metaphysics; the second from biology, Darwin's theory of organic evolution.

The problem that confronted Schopenhauer was one which his generation inherited from Immanuel Kant. Kant had accepted the theory of perception, which maintained that all colors, sounds, and so on were subjective, produced in our minds by causes in the external world. This is approximately the theory that used to be taught in elementary courses in physics: color is caused by light waves in the ether striking our optic nerve endings, setting up a nervous current which is carried to the brain where they turn into red, blue, yellow, or some other color. Analogous theories were formulated to account for other sensations. But at Kant's time the light waves and air waves were not the current talk of philosophers and it was easy to show that the same arguments which made the perceptual qualities subjective could be applied to all qualities of those physical objects that were supposed to be "out there." In fact Bishop Berkeley and David Hume had already demolished the usual accounts of an external world describable in terms of weight, motion, size, and so on. All these terms were shown to be perceptual in origin and hence as subjective as terms of color, sounds, and odor.

That left the philosophers with the world crammed, so to speak, into their skulls. Kant recognized the force of the arguments but realized that a world of perceptual qualities if organized by general principles, such as causal regularity, necessity, quantity, and quality, would do as well as a world of objective properties. For what science needs above all is regularity, dependability, constant measurements; the question of subjectivity or objectivity is for philosophers to worry about. He concluded in his *Critique of Pure Reason* that the causes of our perceptions were unknown and unknowable, things-in-themselves.

If something is unknowable, one should stop talking about it. But people who are willing to stop talking have neither a scientific nor a philosophic bent. The philosophers after Kant insisted on finding out what these things-in-themselves really were. Various proposals were made but none proved entirely satisfactory. At this point, Schopenhauer enters the scene.

Schopenhauer pointed out that everything can be viewed from two angles, from the angle of the outside observer and from the angle of the thing itself. Now the one being which we know from both angles is ourselves. Everything else is known to us only from the outside. We know that to others we are just bodies that talk, move, sleep, are blond or brunette, agreeable or disagreeable— but to ourselves we are aware of desires, hopes, aspirations; in short, we are what we want. It is our wills that characterize us, not our sensations. Sensations are common to all; the will is my own. I am my will when I know myself; I am a collection of perceptual properties, which Schopenhauer called representations (*Vorstellungen*) or ideas to other people. But what is the essence of the will; what does it want? The answer is: Self-perpetuation. And therefore Schopenhauer called it the Will-to-Live. The will has no other purpose and everything it strives for is life, though the covering of its desires may be thought, charity, art, indeed whatever is said by a person to be his motives in acting as he does. It is worth noting that this is the first philosophic statement of Freud's notion that there is a fundamental difference between what we say our motives are and what our real motives are. In Freud this would be called Rationalization. In Marx it was Ideology. Rationalization disguised our sexual drives; ideology, our economic.

Since the will is immediately known only to oneself, one lives in secrecy as if imprisoned within the body. But in its prison the will is always plotting to have its own way. Like a drug it feeds upon its own appeasement and a man who thinks that by giving in to his sexuality he can quiet it, is a victim of his own trickery. Hence the will can never be satisfied, and since the good is the achievement of an end, the will can never achieve goodness. Its activity is the only reality we know at first-hand and it is in essence evil. It is evil because it is mendacious, telling one that "this time will be the last," and then proving that there is no last time. Schopenhauer was not forced to this conclusion. He might have said that since the will-to-live is our only reality behind the perceptual screen, it was in itself an example of what the good really was. He would then have preached the philosophy of the rake and dynamic debauchery. But he did not.

On the contrary, he sought for ways to escape from the tyranny of our will-to-live. Suicide would not do, for it is surrender, not victory. There are only two ways of staying alive and yet conquering. One is through art, for in art no practical problems are instigated; one looks and is absorbed; one listens and becomes part of the music. In art the will is cheated. The second method is through pity. By pity the lot of our fellow men becomes our lot. We take on another's sorrows and live, so to speak, another's life. Our own desires fade away as we identify ourselves with others. This idea he got from the East, having read the Vedas in Latin. His attitude, as Nietzsche called it, was a Nay-saying, a denial of all that we want for the sake of wanting nothing. One can see why certain of the minor details of Schopenhauer's philosophy emerged from his central position. He hated women because they were obviously the greatest temptation to give in to the will-to-live. And he recognized that his philosophy was a pessimism, for at the heart of reality was something evil.

An examination of Schopenhauer's main system would show that it was an exfoliation of the central metaphor of the will as a living being seeking to perpetuate itself. In view of the indisputable fact that some people commit suicide and all can commit it if they wish, the figure of speech did not apply universally. But once it is taken seriously, as if it were not a fiction but a valid description, then the rest is harmonious with it. One could not, however, say that this rest follows logically. Logic has nothing to do with it. Logic might just as well tell us that we ought to give in to the will-to-live and that it is a misnomer to call that which is a real value by the name of evil. Again, logic does not tell us that because the will-to-live is evil we should seek to escape its clutches. It might tell us that escape is impossible and that we are doomed from birth to a tragic end. Schopenhauer said that the original sin was being born. Logic might suggest that that which does not as yet exist could be neither sinful nor virtuous. But enough has been said to suggest that the generating force of this system of ideas is not logic but something else, which might be called lyric coherence.

As an example of a scientific system, let us take Darwin's theory of organic evolution. The problem that Darwin tried to solve was why there were so many species of plants and animals. In Thomas Huxley's *Three Lectures on Evolution* it was pointed out that there were three ways of tackling this problem. The first Huxley called the Miltonic hypothesis: there had always been as many species as there are now. When God created the world, He created at the same time all the kinds of things that now exist. "Now" was, let us say, 1859. The second was the hypothesis of successive creations. This would permit the extinction of certain species. Every once in a while, let us say at the end of a geological epoch, there was a catastrophe which wiped out all life and it was followed by a new creation of new kinds of things. Thus after the extinction of the great reptiles, God created the birds and mammals, and no trace of the dinosaurs was left. There were various ideas about what marked off the several epochs, but, since no one any longer holds to this theory, we can say that Noah's Flood marked the end of one epoch and the various geological periods could be taken as marking the limits of the others. Therefore the new kinds of animals and plants which are found embedded in a layer of rock had no genetic relation to those found in earlier beds but were created afresh when the new layer was created. The third hypothesis was that of evolution, that the species now existing all evolved from earlier species in a manner to be determined. The problem was twofold: Have species evolved? Have they evolved in any determinable order? It is obvious that one can believe that species have evolved but not necessarily believe that there is any determinable order to evolution. Darwin, however, gave an affirmative answer to both questions and, moreover, proposed the means by which the order was achieved. The order given is usually stated as from simple to complex: unicellular organisms, multicellular organisms, invertebrates, vertebrates, reptiles and fishes, birds, mammals. This is a very sketchy outline of the series but it will do for our purposes. One can logically accept this order and still not accept Darwin's account of how it came into being.

To begin with, Darwin made certain observations, of which the most important was that within any species there were always variations. These variations occurred whether the species was under cultivation or in a state of nature. The horticulturalist observes that out of a package of seeds, some plants grow tall, some flowers are paler than others, some plants are sickly. So a man who raises animals knows that he cannot count on all the offspring of a pair being exactly alike in all their features. The same, of course, could be observed in any human family of five or six children. Height, weight, complexion, strength, longevity, along with a lot of other properties, vary in any collection of animals or plants even of the same species.

In the second place, Darwin calculated the number of individuals which would be produced in any species if allowed to increase without obstacles. His most appealing example is that of the elephant, which I quote in his own words:

> The elephant is reckoned the slowest breeder of all known animals, and I have taken some pains to estimate its probable minimum rate of increase; it will be safest to assume that it begins breeding when thirty years old, and goes on breeding till ninety years old, bringing forth six young in the interval, and surviving till one hundred years old; if this be so, after a period of from 740 to 750 years there would be nearly ninteen millions elephants descended from the first pair.[1]

Since each of the descendants of the original elephant pair would also be breeding, and since there can be thought of no time when there was only one primordial pair of elephants, something must have happened to cut down the population? What was it?

Of the many possible answers, the one that Darwin accepted was that of Malthus: there was not enough food for all the possible individuals of a species to get what they needed. Obviously only living animals and plants can produce offspring. Those that survive in each

[1] *Origin of Species*, Chap. III, sec. 3.

98

generation are the parents of the members of the next generation. This is not an observation, nor could it very well be one. The Malthusian principle is an assumption in the context of the *Origin of Species,* though a conclusion to an argument in the context of Malthus' *Essay on the Principle of Population.* I point this out as I am trying to illustrate how an idea grows. Granting then the Malthusian principle, what determines who will get the food he needs?

Darwin, in order to answer this, introduced another premise. Having observed variations within a species, which he thought were accidental, he noticed that some might be useful for getting food and hence for survival. Others might be useless or even harmful. He then either assumed or observed that there is no courtesy, charity, or simple decency among animals and that when there is food enough for only one, he will get it who is the strongest, the quickest, the first on the spot, or the trickiest, and he will not step back and invite his fellows to eat it. But this is equivalent to saying that in a state of nature there is a struggle to survive, and those who do survive are those best equipped to do so. And, to repeat, the superiority of his equipment will be one of the accidental variations.

The next step in the reasoning was Darwin's unfortunate acceptance of the Lamarckian principle, that through use and disuse acquired aptitudes for survival will be reinforced—or allowed to degenerate—and those that are reinforced by use will be inherited by the descendants of such individuals. We know that by gymnastics we can strengthen our muscles and change our conformation if we wish, as by practicing the piano we can limber up our fingers and coordinate what we read on a score with what our fingers do on the keyboard. We also know that if we take no exercise whatsoever, our muscles grow flabby and our fingers lose their agility. So an animal might increase his fleetness of foot by a great deal of running and his nimbleness in avoiding his enemies by learning to hide. Aristotle coined the phrase, "Habit is a second nature," but it is a nature which is acquired; it is by definition not innate. According to the Lamarckian principle such traits could be inherited if they were of use in survival. Hence a strong or fast or clever individual, having increased his speed or strength or cleverness by practice, could pass them on to his children. Neither Lamarck nor Darwin said that any such character could or would be inherited. The modification would have to have some "survival value."

Once this mixture of observation, deduction, and assumption was laid down as premises, one could explain how species might vary in time. They would vary in the direction of those individuals fittest to survive in the struggle for existence. But along with this is the obvious fact that in bisexual species it takes two to make a child. What determines who will mate with whom? Propinquity might do a lot, but in many animal species there is a struggle for mates as well as for food. Males fight with one another in order to have the female that they want. In other species they will court the female and she will presumably pick the one she finds most appealing. In Darwin's word, "A hornless stag or spurless cock would have a poor chance of leaving numerous offspring." Sexual selection then goes along with the entire struggle for existence. But it will be noticed that the existence for which the struggle goes on is that of one's offspring, in brief, that of the species. And since the offspring will have, presumably, the characters of their parents plus accidental variations, the characters of the species as a whole will vary from generation to generation.

This is all very well as an account of what might have happened, but Darwin was even more concerned to prove that it had happened. To do this he called on three kinds of evidence. This evidence was to demonstrate the order in which species had appeared on earth.

First there was the evidence from taxonomy and comparative anatomy. It can be and has been shown that there is a high degree of similarity in all animals of the same family. All mammals from the mouse to man have certain characteristics in common. But in common with some of the nonmammals, a large group have a vertebral column in common. Therefore, on the basis of morphology one can begin with the simplest vertebrate animal and arrange all the other vertebrates so as to form a sort of fanlike pattern with the fish, the reptiles, the birds, the mammals branching out of a single stock. In fact, many textbooks in biology illustrate this in great detail as the Tree of Life.

This would merely show that the Creator had one basic pattern in mind when He created vertebrates. But in the second place Darwin drew on the evidence from embryology. Darwin took over from the German biologist E. E. von Baer the curious Law of Recapitulation, which says that "various parts in the same individual, which are exactly alike during an early embryonic period, become widely different and serve for widely different purposes in the adult state." He quoted Von Baer to the effect that "the embryos of mammalia, of birds, lizards and snakes, probably also of Chelonia, are in the earliest states exceedingly like one another, both as a whole and in the order of development of their parts; so much so, in fact, that we can often distinguish embryos only by their size."

From this one could infer simply that all vertebrates go through similar embryonic stages. But there was another and more telling fact: embryos have certain organs or other characteristics which are lost in the adult animal. The best-known examples are the lower teeth of the cow, which are lost when the cow is an adult, and the gill slits of the human fetus. There are also certain properties which appear in the young animal and are lost later on, the stripes in the whelp of the lion, the spots on the fledgling robin. For the details, which are very numerous, it is essential to refer to the *Origin of Species* (Chap. XIV) itself, for they cannot be reproduced here without extensive quotation, and moreover, many of them have not withstood the assaults of criti-

102

cism. Darwin's own conclusion, drawn from the Law of Recapitulation, was that the embryological history of the individual reproduces the stages through which its species has evolved.

This was still just speculation. The strongest evidence that species had appeared on earth in the order suggested by embryology was that of paleontology. The various strata in which fossils were found showed that the order of the forms ran from the unicellular to the multicellular, that the marine forms came before the terrestrial forms, that reptiles preceded birds and birds preceded mammals, so that there was a rough parallelism between the development of the embryo and the record of the rocks. This was, I repeat, a rough parallelism, and works only for the larger groups of forms. It is safe to say, for that matter, that almost all of Darwin's evidence has been submitted to frequent criticism and most of it has been revised. Many new discoveries in genetics have caused biologists to correct some of his conclusions. Lamarckianism has been dropped. But the general theory that present-day species have evolved from earlier forms remains untouched. What have been corrected are the explanatory details and some of the observations. It should be recalled that Darwin knew nothing of Mendel and could have known nothing of DNA.

Here then is a very rough sketch of a scientific theory, a sketch which indicates what its premises were, what problems it tried to solve, what it assumed, what it inferred. What stood out in nineteenth-century thought was (a) the fact of evolution in the order shown by paleontology, (b) the explanatory formula of the struggle for existence and the survival of the fittest. Men and women argued hotly over the merits of the theory without really knowing much about the evidence. Probably no scientific theory ever stirred up so much heat, for it seemed to violate some of the cardinal principles of religion and also—and this may have been just as important too—reduce man's pride in his humanity. The complete history of the conflict is yet to be written by a historian of ideas, perhaps because to write it would require reading some of the most fulsome literature that has ever disgraced the art of printing. I am not merely referring to such sarcasms as, "If Darwin thinks his grandmother was an ape, he is welcome to do so," but also to such sentimental lines as, "Some call it evolution, others call it God."

Evolution now took on the suffix *ism* and became a mode of explanation. Before one knew, everything evolved. For Herbert Spencer it was not merely organic species that evolved but forms of society, the human mind, art, and religion. For Bergson a half century later it was the *élan vital* that evolved, not because of any struggle for existence, but by a kind of lyric enthusiasm for variety and change. Now, said Bergson, evolution moved in the direction of novelty, and now backwards toward regression. The Law of Recapitulation was a favorite source of new ideas. Some writers maintained that it applied to the human being's mental growth, that the baby was in the most primitive condition, the child at the age of savagery, the youth at, for instance, the stage of Greek culture, and the adult, like the mature animal, was the summation of all that had gone before. Hence educational theorists planned an evolutionistic curriculum; the American child begins with the Indians and moves along through Greece and Rome into colonial history and thence into modernity. Some saw an optimistic note in evolution. Since the animal kingdom seemed to culminate in the best of all animals, man, so the natural process of history would always move from worse to better and when our efforts at reform gave out, we could always turn to evolution to produce what men had been unable to realize. In fact, the spread of evolutionistic ideas could be expounded adequately only in a full-sized book and it is impossible in a sketch of the present sort to do more than hint at it.

But one detail must not be omitted. That is the identification of the later stages of evolution with the better, and the earlier with the potentially, but not actually, good. Not only was the course of evolution toward the more adequate adjustment to the environment, as manifested in man and the marine mammals, but it was also identified with moral progress. People actually believed what now seems incredible to some of us, that in time men would grow better and better and reach a very high, if not the highest, point of culture. Just as there was a kind of fatuous pride in being human rather than formic or leonine, so there was an equally and more condemnable pride in Occidental society as the acme of the historical pyramid. In accordance with this, the societies of preliterate people were called primitive, backward, undeveloped—and it became "the white man's burden" to make them advanced, forward-looking, and developed. It was up to us, the white men of the Occident, to help our little brown brothers attain to our position of greatness. We are reaping the fruits of this drive now in the mid-twentieth century. A more consistent point of view was that of Spencer himself, who, as a Lamarckian, argued that since evolution was a law of nature, in time the backward people would either evolve or perish.

There was therefore an ingression into a theory (which started out to be simply a theory of how species became diversified) of notions of social reform, and some men who believed in the superiority of nature to art interpreted the natural as the animal. They were opposed by others who maintained that it was human nature, not plain nature, that was involved. That there is an animal side to human nature is undeniable, and the debate hinged upon the weight that would be given it. If we are simply hairless apes, then the life of the hairy ape might well be taken as a model. If, on the other hand, our particularly well-developed brain differentiated us enough from the apes to make us a new variety of primate, then we might possibly discover a way of life that was essentially human and not animal. The flight from society, the return to nature, the simple life—all were slogans that sprang from an emphasis on our animal side. The crux of the matter, which is usually overlooked, is the situation in which our problems arise.

Do they arise in the context of animality or in that of beings that are a mixture of two natures? If we wish to live like animals, then we can easily enough destroy our churches, our schools, our libraries, our whole economic structure. We would then fight for our food and mates, let the sick and the congenitally weak die of starvation or weakness and produce no children. We might by both natural and selective breeding produce a race of muscular football players. The extreme alternative would seem to be either a purely rational life or one given to mystic contemplation. But this seems impossible. We might of course make allowances for our animal nature while keeping it in control. And this is precisely what we find in history. We see there an undulation between savagery and civilization. At the time of writing, the accent seems to be on savagery both in the extent to which so-called civilized peoples are engaged in warfare and in the rejection of the arts of civilization on a wide scale. The Hippie has a good reason for his flight from hypocrisy and cruelty. But to flee is not to solve the problem from which one is escaping. Oddly enough, the Hippie lives in a society of his own and shows great sympathy for the needs of his fellows in that society. The ancient Cynics were Hippies also, but they fled from other Cynics as well as from the Establishment. If you are going to have a society, even of the unwashed lying about on mattresses, you will soon find that you are developing rules. And rules are the bricks out of which society is built.

There is no need to despair about this situation. The books of Kings and Plutarch's *Lives* make one realize that similar situations have existed in the past and that the opponents of savagery have frequently won out. This is not a historical law and I should not like to be interpreted as maintaining that it is one. At the present time, the nation as a social and political unit is on the way out, though it will remain a political unit for some time to come. Someone some day will argue that our primary duty is not to the nation but to the human race as a whole, that every war is a civil war, and that there are no frontiers. I can hardly be sure that such a day will arrive, for all life may well be exterminated when the great powers decide to exterminate it. Our survival depends upon a set of ideas which religion might have been expected to propagate. But religions have been more interested in their own powers and preserving them.

Thus we can see that in this particular instance the systematic character of a theory is the consistency of the evidence that is used to demonstrate its truth. That is, there was no inner contradiction in the sentences used by Darwin in the *Origin of Species*. Psychologically it seemed plausible to some of the people who read it and to a great many people who had not read it but had read about it. The arguments against it came from two sources: from biologists themselves who tried to verify some of Darwin's supporting ideas by observation, and from religiously minded people who thought that it contradicted the book of Genesis. It is worth pointing out that some people felt compelled to believe both and hence had recourse to the ancient technique of interpreting the Bible allegorically. The days of Creation then turned into geological epochs; God's hand was seen in the evolutionary process, and there was talk of reconciling the Miltonic and the Darwinian hypotheses. Such talk came to nothing, especially when it was realized that there was much in Darwinism that required correction. And since the Adversary was under attack from his own forces, that seemed to strengthen the point of view of religion.

The systems which we have sketched were networks of ideas tied together either by logical consistency or by literary harmony. But one can also build a system by a single technique of description. The most familiar example of this is mechanism as utilized in the physical sciences and transferred to the social sciences. The mechanistic technique rests upon the methodological rule of explaining everything that happens as due to the operation of material causes. To define what is meant by a material cause is far from easy. Are light rays and air waves material causes? To escape from the problem one imagined that the former were waves in something known as the ether and the latter as waves in the material, air. Historically, matter was believed to be that which had mass and which moved according to the laws of motion as framed by Newton. This technique reduced or eliminated from the subject matter of the sciences all the sensory qualities. They were relegated to the world of psychology; and the psychologist, as if embarrassed by these immaterial beings, denied their existence as anything other than effects of muscles, glands, biochemistry, electric currents in the brain. That an effect is as real as a cause did not seem to trouble the psychologist of this type. When the mechanist was dealing with social problems, he had to find some material correlative to human desires, antagonisms, aggressions, and so on, that seemed to be responsible for the things that men did. The human body was a material object and so was food, which it needed, and the land on which the food was grown. The power that ran its factories was also material, whether it was water power, steam, oil, or electricity. The people who operated the factories were also dependent on food and land and power. If, then, one could discover the causal efficacy of these material essentials, one would have found out why human beings behave as they do. It was Karl Marx who, by combining what he knew of economics with what he took over from Hegel's theory of dialectical evolution, was able to construct the first important materialistic, or mechanistic, system of history. By transforming Hegel's dialectics into the pattern of history and making history a matter of economics, he made a system by unity of method. In its most extreme form it would assert that all human thought is determined by economic causes. But not even Marx held it in so extreme a form. This was a flaw in the system's unity but a tribute to its founder's common sense. Unfortunately for the extreme form of mechanistic history, men's thoughts may modify their behavior. Even the most materialistic economist had to grant that economic causes could operate only through human feelings, desires, wishes, and perhaps aspirations. Hopes for the future have been the most potent motives of both the Russians and the Chinese. But hopes do not have mass and they care nothing for the laws of motion. The mechanistic method worked best where it arose, in mechanics. When an attempt was made to use it in other fields, the method was analogical at best and the unity of the system more apparent than real.

There are other forms of system which should be mentioned. First, there is the system of ethical unity, according to which all multiplicity works for the attainment of *The Good*. This is usually a philosophic, not a scientific, system. But at the same time, when scientists explained change on a teleological basis, their ends were goods, as in Aristotle. No one today would explain motion as purposive. But when one is studying biology or psychology or even sociology, one finds it difficult to avoid explaining what happens teleologically. When a bird is seen gathering bits of straw, how is one to avoid saying that it is *in order* to build its nest? And analogously it is easier to say that the heart supplies blood for the rest of our economy than to explain what it does on the basis of antecedent mechanical causes. The person who is interested in the function of the heart as part of the human organism will explain it on the basis of what the heart is for. The cardiologist will isolate it from those parts of the body to which it is not immediately related and describe it as a pump. When men try to use the teleological method as a universal explanatory technique, they are forced into myth or allegory, if they do not stop short at analogy. Nevertheless, the historian of ideas will have to take account of teleological systems as well as of any other type.

Neither the history of mechanism nor of teleology as explanatory methods has ever been thoroughly studied. In both cases a basic metaphor had been expanded to cover events for which it was not devised. It throws little light on human relations to describe them only in biochemical terms, for though biochemistry may be at the basis of our behavior, it is biochemistry translated into terms of human ideas, because the problems that people try to solve are not on the biochemical level. That is, when two men are engaged in commercial rivalry or political strife or athletic competition, what they do certainly has biochemical determinants, just as it has social and psychological determinants. But in all these cases the men are aware of seeking a purpose, even an ideal. They are not aware of their adrenal glands, their electrochemical brain waves, or their economic status at the moment they are running a race. They want to win. Conversely when a planet moves round the sun, its behavior can be fully described in terms of the Law of

Gravitation in which only masses and distance need be calculated. Nothing is gained in astronomy by saying that the planets declare the glory of God or that they move around the sun in almost perfect circles because they are striving to approximate geometric perfection or because each planet is inhabited by a guiding spirit which drives it along its path. The extension of purpose to the unconscious, the inanimate, is an illegitimate extension unless it is recognized to be a metaphor. But whatever the truth of the matter, men as intelligent as we are used this technique and felt satisfied when they had projected purpose into events in which we find none.

Such projections are not unusual. When the Stoics talked about cosmic harmony, they were projecting a characteristic of the Stoic Sage into the universe as a whole. The Stoic Sage had a mind undisturbed by emotion—it was never upset. All his faculties worked together to produce or at least to permit the free exercise of his reason. So all the parts of the Cosmos cooperated in harmony to form a sublime spectacle for the man fit to observe it. The whole which the Stoic believed in was an aesthetic whole, but in Greek thought the aesthetic and the moral were fused into one ideal, the admirable, the beautiful-and-good. In concrete terms it was the submission of all things to a single law enunciated by a single lawgiver, God. But what was this law? That was exactly what the philosopher had to find out. In most Occidental religions the law was the triumph of Goodness. Even when Evil seemed to have the upper hand, the religious man, whether Jew or Christian, whether Catholic or Protestant, agreed with the Stoic in maintaining that apparent evils are real goods. "Though He slay me, yet will I trust in Him."

There were other alternatives, as there always are, to the law being ethical. There might be a law such as that of equilibrium. For instance, one might say that the universe exists to preserve a balance between oxygen and carbon dioxide, and hence plants breathe out oxygen for the animals to breathe in and animals exhale carbon dioxide for the plants to absorb. This could be elaborated into a thesis like Emerson's Law of Compensation. There could be imagined a rule that the world's events proceeded as rewards for human goodness and punishment for human crimes. In fact, drought and rainfall have already been explained as God's punishment on men for their wickedness, as the biblical flood was due to God's repentance for having created so wicked a race as man. The general idea behind such reflections is the centrality of the human species in the cosmos. According to this idea everything that exists exists for the use of mankind, but mankind must make proper use of it. Yet this was not the only system which was anthropocentric. For instance, the Manicheans believed that mankind was central in the cosmos, but also that what happened in history was determined by the interaction of two deities, one good and one bad.

My reason for dwelling on this is that there is a tendency to argue that if a man maintained proposition P, he must also have maintained proposition Q, if Q either presupposes P or follows logically from P. But the historian is engaged in relating what happened, not what might have happened or what should have happened. Lamarck or Darwin perhaps should have observed that athletes' children do not have biceps that are bigger than those of other people's children. Weissmann cut off the tails of twenty generations of rats and found that the rats of the twenty-first generation had tails just as long, or short, as those of the first generation. Jews ever since the days of Abraham have had their foreskins cut off, but their male children are still born with foreskins. Both of these observations could be explained away, the first, as Bernard Shaw dealt with it, namely that rats' tails serve no vital purpose; the second, that God has ordained circumcision and hence there must be something to circumcise. The historian would note such details, for they tell him a good bit about how ideas change or fail to change.

The element of wishful thinking is more potent in the history of ideas than that of logic. In the early eighteenth century biologists believed that either the father or the mother, but not both, was responsible for the traits of their children. But when a man named Maupertuis came along, he pointed out that if this were true, then all children should resemble either their fathers or their mothers but not both, whereas they resemble now one, now the other. Thus he refuted those who derived all characters from the father's sperm or the mother's egg and pointed out that both apparently were needed to make a child. Thus an idea that had been held in one form or another since the days of Aristotle was blown to pieces. Anyone might have raised Maupertuis' objection; but when one reads the disputes of the ovists and the animalculists, one realizes that nothing is more hidden than the obvious. To see this is one of the benefactions of the history of ideas.

It does not look as if ideas, then, should always be thought of as integrated into a larger system of ideas unless they are actually presented in such a context. There is no thesis of Darwin's that was not broached in earlier times and separately. The very term "species" had been questioned in the eighteenth century. However, systems resemble another common way of treating ideas; that is, the way of relating them to periods, times, ages, and to the so-called spirit that is supposed to belong to an age. We shall now turn to that.

·6·

Ages and Times—Periodization

One of the most popular ways of explaining the changes in ideas as history moves along is that of attributing the nature of ideas to the age or period of which they are supposed to be characteristic. It is obvious that a historian, whether a historian of ideas, of politics, of economics, of art or of religion cannot record everything that has ever occurred in chronological order. History has to be broken up into centuries or shorter lengths of time to make the recital of events less cumbersome. The most familiar example is the division of Occidental history into Antiquity, the Dark Ages, the Middle Ages, and Modern Times, each of which times had been further divided according to the tastes and interests of the historian. But the technique with which we are dealing in this chapter is somewhat different. It consists in first looking for and usually finding some peculiar property that characterizes the ages individually and second in using that quality as the cause of what goes on during the age in question. Readers of Spengler, Sorokin, and Toynbee are familiar with this technique. But as a matter of fact it goes back much further and was anticipated by Hesiod and the mythographers.

According to Hesiod each age but one was named after a metal. They were the Golden, Silver, Bronze, and Iron Ages, the names of which obviously connoted decreasing value. Between the Age of Bronze and the Iron Age, our own, came the Age of Heroes. The people of the Golden Age were happy, being merry and fond of feasting; the earth produced its fruits spontaneously, so that no work was needed in order to live; and there was no war or violence of any kind. This period was the best that has ever existed, the best morally as well as economically. From then on there was degeneration up to the Age of Heroes. The Golden Race died out; why, was not disclosed by Hesiod. It was followed by the Silver Race. These men were not descended from their predecessors but were an entirely new creation. They were bad, being foolish and childish, insolent to one another and impious. Hence they were destroyed by Zeus. There followed the third race, the Race of Bronze. They were physically and mentally superior to the second race, but they were also warlike and they destroyed themselves because of their belligerency. Then came the Age of Heroes. This was the race that produced the men who fought the Trojan War. In spite of their warlike nature, they did not die out, but were translated to the Islands of the Blessed where Kronos rules over them. There they live in happiness and plenty. After them came our own race, that of iron. "Would that I were not among the fifth race," says Hesiod, "but had either died before or were born afterwards." This race is full of anxiety and will degenerate as the years go on. When they are "born with greying temples," they will be wiped out. Their condition is the antithesis of that of the Golden Race, for they live in suffering, toil, internal and external war. Force will supplant justice, and good passions will be supplanted by evil. Finally this race too will disappear.

Hesiod's account is of interest to us in spite of its incoherence, because it asserts that the character of an age determines that of its inhabitants. The people of the Golden Age are happy because the earth bears its fruits spontaneously, not because they have decided not to fight or be envious or whatever might be thought to be the cause of unhappiness. Each succeeding race, except that of the Heroes, is what it is because of the period in which it lives. The age itself has a character—for example, golden or silver—and that makes the people of the age either happy or unhappy. Though the steady course of degeneration is only hinted at in Hesiod, later writers were to smooth it out so that the deterioration of humanity would be constant. In our own times writers have argued in a similar fashion. For instance, the people of the eighteenth century were rational because they were living in an Age of Reason or because they "expressed" the rationality of the age they lived in. The artists of the sixteenth century, again, were bold and dynamic, painted and sculpted turmoil and passion because they were expressing the spirit of the Baroque Age. We today are said to be tormented by nightmares of internecine war because we are living in an Age of Anxiety, and hence painters must paint pictures which are nightmarish and sculptors must distort the human form out of any recognition. In another version we are told that artists must eliminate all reference to perceptual reality and give us purely abstract form, since the individual is lost in the mass-mind, a mind which, it seems to be forgotten, is the product of some historian's imagination.

The early Christian Fathers took the six days of creation for their paradigm of history. The question of why there were six days instead of one or some other number was answered through the method of number symbolism. But a correlation was made as early as the fifth century by St. Augustine between the six days of creation and the day of rest and the seven ages of man. The life-cycle was used, as it was to be used by an indefinite number of later historians, as a model for history. The first day, on which God said, "Let there be light," corresponded to infancy and each successive day corresponded to each of the ages of a human individual, e.g., boyhood, youth, maturity, senescence, until the seventh which was to be the Cosmic Sabbath, the Age of the Second Coming. This pattern of history indicates St. Augustine's belief that human beings as a whole go through a predetermined course of history over which they have no more control than a child has over his immaturity or an old man over his senility. The period, for instance, when David was ruling was the period of youth and corresponds to the fourth day of creation when the stars were made. "For how could the splendor of a reign be more clearly symbolized than by the perfection of the sun? And the light of the moon means the people obedient to its kingdom, like the synagogue itself, and the stars mean the princes and all things established as if in the firmament in the stability of the kingdom. Its evening fell with the sins of the kings for which that people deserved to be taken captive and to serve in slavery" (*De Genesi contra Manichaeos*, I, 23; *PL* 34, col. 190ff.). There is a mixture here of two themes, the theme of historical determinism and that of human free will. Did the kings sin because the age was bound to pass into a new and less desirable condition as youth passes into manhood? Or were they free not to sin? The answer to the second question was given in the *City of God* where we learn that after the Fall man lost his power not to sin (*non possumus non peccare*).

St. Augustine's outline of history was repeated throughout the Middle Ages, but in the twelfth century a new set of ages was invented by Joachim of Floris. To his way of thinking there were three ages, corresponding to the three Persons of the Trinity, a pattern that had been suggested before and was surely very tempting to Christian thinkers. For until the Incarnation it was easy to maintain that men were living in the Age of the Father and that after that they were living in the Age of the Son. Why should there not be a third age corresponding to the Age of the Holy Spirit? In the first age, according to Joachim, men were living "according to the flesh"; in the second, "between the flesh and the spirit"; in the third they will live according to the spirit alone. They will then become purely spiritual beings. Joachim, moreover, divides each age into three parts and carries the triadic division throughout and in several way. Thus in the first age, the laity were predominant; in the second, the clergy; and in the third it will be the monks. We cannot go into all the details of this interesting philosophy of history but must again content ourselves by pointing out that the age has the characteristics in question and the individuals living in that age have them only insofar as the age determines them.

In the eighteenth century the paradigm of ages became more popular than previously. Vico and Herder believed, like Joachim, in three ages; Condorcet in nine; Turgot, Saint-Simon, and Comte returned to three. These ages like those that had preceded them were chronologically ordered and were homogeneous. The novelty in Vico's thought was that the spirit of his heroic, religious, and humanistic ages was pervasive of everything that happened in them. Vico was a student of comparative law, to which he added an interest in mythology and literature. He seems to have been the first to attempt a detailed analysis of his ages to see how their "spirits" would express themselves in law, in literature, in religion, and generally in customs. Herder took the same point of view but he was hardly the scholar that Vico was, being more narrow in his concern. He had, in spite of that, much more influence than Vico until our own times, probably because more people read German than Italian. In the case of Comte, as of Vico, the character of an age was identical with the way people thought. In the first age, the theological, they thought like children, investing all things with deities whose will produced effects. In the second, the metaphysical, they thought like adolescents, divesting the gods of their personality and thinking in terms of abstract beings. In the third, just beginning to be realized, the positivistic age, they will think like descriptive scientists and believe in the reality only of what can be scientifically perceived. For Comte all history followed this law of the three stages, making the future as inevitable in character as the past. But he was willing to admit that in each age there were hangovers from preceding ages and anticipations of the future.

No one of these patterns was purely descriptive. Some, like Hesiod's for instance, are primitivistic, holding the first age to be the best; others, like Joachim's are anti-primitivistic, maintaining that the best is yet to be. Since the basic metaphor in most of these cases is the life-cycle, a good deal depends on whether the thinker has a high opinion of old age or a higher opinion of childhood. And this is sometimes, though not necessarily, associated with

one's attitude toward the intellect. The supposed inno-
cence and innate wisdom of the child has led some writers
to think of all history as degeneration. On the other hand,
some have believed that it is better to be an adult than
a child, and hence have taken a more optimistic view of
history. In Spengler the history of a people ended in death,
beginning with what he called the Faustian period of
creativity and passing into the contemplative Apollonian
stage of middle age. Thus, all three possibilities have been
seriously entertained. But what it literally means for a
whole culture to be born or to die is seldom made clear.
Nor could it be made clear unless, by death, one means
the extermination of all the people sharing that culture.
In the Old Testament and in Greek history we do read of
cities being razed and their inhabitants slaughtered. But
to say that, for instance, Greek or Roman or Hebraic
culture had died out is simply untrue. The men who wrote
the Greek literary and scientific works are indeed dead
and so are the authors of the Bible. But the culture itself, though changed, is dead only in the sense that an
adult is a dead child.

I shall now cite two examples of periodization, those
of Comte and of Hegel. These are the two most influential in modern times.

Comte, as I have said, favored the basic metaphor of
the life-cycle, though he stopped short of death. History
was divided into three periods: childhood, youth, and
maturity. In the childhood of the race, by which he really
meant of Occidental man, all change was attributed to
a will or group of wills belonging to gods. This period was

therefore called by him "the theological period" and its dominant members were tribal priests. The priests are those men who alone know how to influence the gods by sacrifice and prayer, by festivals and dances and hymns, and it is interesting to observe that Comte realized that one does not argue with a volition. One uses the logic of persuasion, not the logic of conviction. As the child passes into youth, he depersonalizes the wills that run the universe and calls them forces, entelechies, essences, and principles, believing that abstract entities are more sophisticated than volitions. This period is that of metaphysics, and the metaphysicians are the dominant group in it. But when the adolescent grows to maturity, he sees that these forces are just as naïve as the divine wills in which he believed as a child and he now relies only on what he can observe with his sense organs. The perceptual world in all its order and regularity is now the real world. This period Comte called "the positivistic period" and its dominant members are the scientists, in which group Comte included the engineers. This total conception is one in which historical periods are characterized by the typical mode of explanation used in them. The theological period explains on the analogy of human action: if a man wishes to do something, his will is the cause of what he does. It is a cause in the sense of something which makes the event to happen. It is as if a craftsman were taking a piece of wood and carving it by his muscles and will power into some pattern of which he had foreknowledge.

So in the metaphysical period the causes of things are

the objects of knowledge. Only now these causes lose their anthropomorphic air. They become immaterial essences which cannot be observed and the existence of which can only be inferred from the assumption that something or other is needed to cause phenomena from behind the scenes. Thus naïve people will say that a stone falls to earth because of gravity, or that iron rusts because it has an affinity for oxygen. Comte's point is that the word "because" in these sentences is meaningless; for the adult scientist realizes that there is no such "cause" as gravity or chemical affinity; there are only observable events that regularly occur when certain things happen. He is satisfied with the statement of the conditions under which these events occur and it must be put in the language of perception.

For Hegel the periods were defined by the mode of consciousness which prevailed in them, not by the mode of explanation. This mode of consciousness was an inherent quality of the periods, as indeed it was also in Vico. Hegel thought of all history as associated with three regions of the earth, the Orient, the Mediterranean Basin, and Northern Europe. Each region had its own peculiar spiritual constitution which appeared, as in Vico, in everything that its inhabitants did. In the Orient all political power was concentrated in the hands of one man, the despot. There were no limits to the despot's power and the people counted for nothing. Art was vague and atmospheric; religion was pantheistic. Since all art is fused with religion, according to Hegel, the vagueness of Ori-

ental art comes from the same source as the pantheistic
ideas which it attempts to symbolize. The symbols to us
are ambiguous and "as we enter for the first time the
world of ancient Persian, Indian, or Egyptian figures and
imaginative conceptions we experience a certain feeling
of uncanniness, we enter at any rate in a world of problems."[1] Just as political power is limitless, so are the divine
and the beautiful. It was one of Hegel's basic principles
that by obstinate self-assurance one turned into one's opposite, the master becoming a slave to his slaves in order
to become more of a master, the slave becoming the
master of his master. This exclusive emphasis on the indefinite led to its opposite in the democracies of Greece
where power was pulverized and each individual was sovereign. So in art the individual human figure became the
ideal and in religion the infinite divinity of the Orient
was split up into hundreds of anthropomorphic gods, to
the point where every spring and river, every mountain,
every grove of trees had its presiding deity. But this too
could not last. And by a historical law of development the
indefiniteness of the Orient was synthesized with the
concreteness of Greece and Rome and became the personal monarch of Prussia where the Oriental despotism
was mitigated by the claims of the people on their king.
So in religion there was retained from classical antiquity
the personality of the gods, but it was fused with the
universality of pantheism to form Christian (by which

[1] *Philosophy of Art*, trans. F. P. B. Osmaston (London, 1920),
Vol. II, p. 14.

127

Hegel meant Lutheran) monotheism. In art the humanity of the Greeks was spiritualized humanity, a synthesis
of symbolic and concrete representation. A statue of
Apollo looks like a man, but it is also a symbol of light
and healing. In modern European art both would be
clear yet unified.

Hegel obviously is not thinking of any cause external
to human affairs, such as physico-chemical phenomena,
droughts or floods, sun spots, famine or glut, as determinants of human history. He maintained that history
had its own laws, which were as a matter of fact universal
laws, laws of the dialectical process. History was to be
understood "from within." And all man's interests had
to be considered, whether they were of a purely philosophic or scientific nature or were political or aesthetic.
There was, as all the books point out, a metaphysical principle which acted as the soul of history, that which Hegel
called *the Idea*. Historical evolution was the evolution
of the Idea which could be traced as well in logic as in
the consciousness of the individual. The later periods grew
out of the early by an inherent law of development, again
like a child growing out of infancy not by reacting to an
external and foreign environment, but because of its own
inner nature. The infant either grows into childhood or
dies. The death of childhood is its fulfillment in boyhood.
Once again we see the metaphor of biological growth at
play.

At the same time one should not overlook the fact that
Hegel's theory was a theory ultimately concerned with

the history of ideas themselves and not of their causes. His logic illustrates how he utilized the traditional thesis that all determination is negation (*Omnis determinatio est negatio*). What an assertion asserts is the negation of its contradictory. To say, "This is a cat," is to deny that it is a dog, a rat, a cow, or anything else, or, in the jargon of the schools, a noncat. That obviously is why he put a temporal dimension into his logic and tried to show how the logical sequence of the most abstract ideas runs parallel to the historical development of specific ideas—philosophical, political, religious, aesthetic. He made his logical principle into a historical law. And just as he believed that any assertion "implies" its contradictory, so he believed that any historical period turns into its antithesis, in the way that what he called Oriental despotism turned into Greek democracy, and Greek democracy turned into Northern European constitutional monarchy. In despotism, all power is concentrated in the hands of one man; in democracy, power is given to all; in a constitutional monarchy, both one man and the people as a whole share in the powers of government.

The weakness of all theories that make the spirit of an age a determinant is that they seem to presuppose the existence of this spirit as apart from the individual human beings affected by it. But clearly, if you eliminate the human beings from an age, there is no discoverable spirit of that age. I say "discoverable," for it may be retorted that the spirit of an age is only discoverable in the people whom it informs, but that nevertheless it exists apart from them, just as color or shape is not identical with the things that are colored or have shapes. The spirit of an age is presumably found by examining what people have said and written between certain years. If those people contradicted one another, then this spirit would be in a state of inner contradiction. And if there were a noticeable amount of contradiction then, one would imagine, there would be no spirit at all. The question boils down to the amount of homogeneity that exists during a given period and how it is produced.

The first of these problems can be solved only by examining the literature of any period. And I may say with some assurance that no age that I have ever examined, including the thirteenth century, the so-called Age of Reason, and the fifth century B.C. in Athens, has been without its inner antagonisms as far as ideas are concerned. The writers of the great Athenian period can be proved to have been split by the antagonism between writers like Aristophanes and Euripides, between Aristophanes and Socrates, between the Sophists and the Traditionalists; after all, both Anaxagoras and Socrates were prosecuted, and the latter executed, because of what they taught. The thirteenth century, which has been called the most united of all times, was split between the Thomists and the Scotists, the Dominicans and the Franciscans, and this not on trivial grounds, but on the very nature of God. Politically no one would say that Innocent III unified Europe; quite the contrary. Aesthetically it was the age of the great Gothic cathedrals, but it is easy enough to distinguish between Italian and French Gothic, French and English Gothic. But such arguments seldom prevail, for people who believe in ages and their guardian spirits always retort that such variations are superficial and the underlying similarity is identity.

In spite of this there are in fact seeds of uniformity which are discoverable and which help to explain why historians like to talk in terms of ages. First is the human desire for conformity, for social approbation. It is a common human desire to find others who agree with one and to agree with those who are famous or well known in the community. A great poet soon has followers and if so, they will accept his ideas as well as his music. The same is true of a great painter or architect. The imitators of Henri Rousseau, of Picasso, and more recently of Pollock, are legion. What makes such men great is another matter: sometimes it is loud praise by critics, at other times a sincerely felt emotion of their artistic power. There is no logical tie between a man's artistic skill and the truth of his ideas, but there is a psychological tie. The ideas of Alexander Pope, as expressed in his *Essay on Man* or the *Essay on Criticism*, strike me as false, but I also think they are superbly expressed. What he had to say in these poems was pretty widely accepted and was quoted—and still is—just as widely. Pope's ability as a poet attracted people to his ideas and, because it is pleasant to agree with a man who is a great poet, a circle of Pope's admirers was formed. We have seen this in our own time in the cenacle of admirers of

Sartre, Camus, Lévi-Strauss, and Marcuse. None of these men are trivial figures. But let it be noted that our age is the age of all of them, and not of one only, and that they are far from being unanimous about any issue.

In the second place there is a strong desire on the part of many, indeed most, people to belong to a group. Human beings are gregarious animals and though some of them prefer relative solitude and detachment, that is usually a preference that comes from education. One has to learn to prefer it. For the human family with its prolongation of infancy, the dominance of parents, the school which emphasizes *esprit de corps*, the Church with its accent on being one mystic body, business associations, labor unions, fraternities of one sort or another, drive one (the American perhaps more than any other) to feel the need for companionship. This has reached the point where "togetherness" has become a joke.

But one of the binding forces of a group is its supposed program, and a program is always a cluster of ideas. Like the Creed in Christian churches, it has to be accepted and its acceptance qualifies one for membership in the group. Even nations set up a sort of creed when they print mottos on their coats of arms or adopt emblems which stand for mottos, the eagle with olive branches in one talon and arrows in the other. For some reason or other, people have to put their hopes into words, as if verbal expression gave a hope more solidity than it would have if expressed merely in action. The probability is that fear and hatred are the most powerful social cements yet discovered. There is no jealousy in either hatred or fear, whereas there is always some when two people love or hope for the same thing. That, however, belongs to the psychologist or the sociologist to decide, not to the historian of ideas.

The third point that should be made is that membership in a group makes for stability. Insofar as society as a whole is a single group, to that extent it will do everything in its power to preserve its stability. No society is ever going to commit suicide, though it may be murdered. But since its stability will depend upon its unity, and since its unity will be largely, if not entirely, a matter of ideals, a society will incorporate an idea which it will also express in the form of an idea. We see this on a grand scale when the nations of the capitalist world call themselves the Free World, as if they all stood for the same kind of freedom and stood for it to the same degree. What the phrase concretely stands for is capitalism in some form or other as a defense against Russian or Chinese Communism. But anyone who joins in a crusade loses a large amount of his freedom *ipso facto*. The idea of freedom itself has an interesting history, which Professor Mortimer Adler has outlined for us in his *The Idea of Freedom*. If, then, our desire for stability is satisfied by belonging to a stable group and if that group stands for certain ideals, we shall accept these ideals and help their realization quite as wholeheartedly as if we had discovered them for ourselves.

This may suffice to throw some light on how periods

acquire uniformity. There are, however, certain criticisms that should be made.

First, there is much more actual heterogeneity within periods than has been admitted by those historians who believe in their importance. At the time of writing (1968), there is open conflict of ideas within the United States, ideas about races, about economics, about art, and about theology. We have our racists both black and white, the former maintaining that every white man is an enemy, the latter maintaining that every Negro is inferior morally and intellectually to any white man. We have economic reformers who run all the way from advocating more governmental control of industry to out-and-out Communism, with nineteenth-century *laisser-faire* standing by. In artistic circles one finds everything from traditional naturalistic painting and sculpture to Op Art and Pop Art, abstract expressionism and concrete expressionism, and on the far left—the Triumph of the Fortuitous. In theology we have all shades of opinion as well, running from Catholics who believe that *extra Ecclesiam nulla salus* to those who believe that God is dead. The one pervasive idea that might be abstracted from this hodge-podge of opinion and practice is that of diversity. But if one thinks that Americans actually believe in diversity and tolerance, he is wrong. Each group believes that it is in the right, and some will use force against opposing groups. Wholesale arson and looting are not done in a spirit of toleration.

Second, the clashes in opinion that have always existed

give rise to new problems and to new emphases. If all people agreed on everything, there would obviously be no occasion to change, for even if the application of an idea is a failure, one can always say that it was badly applied. This is not sarcasm. We have all seen too many instances of it, from the spiritualist who says that the seance did not work because of the presence of skeptics to the legislator who points to the wickedness of the public rather than to the weakness of his statute (witness prohibition). Intellectual progress has always come about through dispute, as the history of science shows very clearly. A scientific idea is put on probation: critics argue about its weaknesses; its proponents correct—or try to correct—these weaknesses when real, and in time a new theory is advanced. The debate between Pasteur and Bastian on biogenesis is a beautiful illustration of this. Each step in the argument was either a demonstration on Bastian's part of what might be a weakness in Pasteur's method or a correction by Pasteur following Bastian's lead. In science this can be illustrated more forcefully than in other fields, since scientific statements are always statements of fact and hence controllable by experimentation. But where, as in philosophy, aesthetic theory and theology or in the social sciences, experimentation is impossible, assertions are either propositions of policy or ostensible propositions of fact which conceal propositions of policy—or only more or less probable statistical generalizations about the past, though sometimes the very recent past. Such problems are sel-

dom solved; people grow tired of them and they are rejected as unimportant, trivial, out of date, or even
meaningless.

Sometimes the clash in opinion generates new emphases. For instance, in the nineteenth century the relation between the mind and the body was a burning
question in both philosophic and psychological circles.
The technique of determinism in the natural sciences
seemed to be essential for any reliable scientific theory.
Hence the question must be faced whether the body was
the cause of the mind's various "states," or whether there
was such a thing as mental causation, as in hypnosis, or
whether there could be causal interaction between the
two, bodily conditions sometimes determining mental,
mental sometimes determining physical. The decision
made regarding determinism also affected the decision
that would be made regarding freedom of the will. If
all mental conditions were determined by bodily conditions, then whatever decisions a man made were in the
last resort the result of bodily conditions: his health,
his food, his sex, drugs, pain, his age, and the like. And
it was sometimes asserted that if a man's will was not
free to choose between A and not-A, then there was
no meaning to such concepts as that of right and wrong,
good and bad. After a period during which the word
"mind" was ruled out of court and "behavior" substituted for it, the mind-body problem was shelved, but
the question of determinism vs. free will remained. Only
now it was no longer the question of the freedom of an

ethereal mental entity, but of behavior, an event. This being so, it became legitimate to turn to the calculus of probability, and since determinism was modified even in physics (though in a very special case) it was no longer incorrect to introduce it into psychology. A volition could be seen to be more or less free depending on the circumstances under which it was made. In any event, chance was now a respectable member of the scientific community and one no longer believed it to be simply another name for our ignorance. The historian of ideas could trace the history of the idea of freedom of the will from the ancient philosophers who took it for granted (the Epicureans) and their debates with those who flatly denied it (the Stoics) through the Church Fathers and their debates with the Pelagians, the triumph of the proponents of freedom during the late Middle Ages, the weakening of the theory as physical science began to develop in the Renaissance, through the disputes about the mind-body problem in the seventeenth century, to the disputes about the very existence of the mind raised by such men as William James and, later, J. B. Watson, its resurgence as a result of the work of the Freudians, and our contemporary mass of conflicting opinions.

A more serious criticism of the notion of periods and ages is that it usually makes ideas independent of human beings and human interests. It might perhaps be argued that mathematics develops in a world of its own, within which the desires of men are unknown. But as far as all other ideas are concerned, they are engendered by human beings and nurtured by them as well as combatted by them. And all this in the world that surrounds us, the world of physical laws. I am not denying that random curiosity has often played a part in the history of ideas. A man may simply wonder what would happen if. . . . Or he might speculate about the truth of something that he had read. He might, for instance, have been reading Plutarch's *Lives* and wondered why the ancients were so convinced of the truth of omens that they would base even important decisions upon them. At the same time they would reinterpret an omen in order to make the future more propitious. What was there about ancient Mediterranean religion that could convince people that a flight of two ravens over their heads or a clap of thunder or the shape of a bullock's liver could actually foretell what was about to happen if they—not everybody in general, but they—were to cross a bridge or shout defiance at an enemy or cast a vote? Did they think that the cosmic laws in which all educated Greeks and Romans believed would be adjusted to their interests? Did they think that whatever happened was the result of chance, and that they could somehow sway it? Plutarch takes omens for granted and does not answer this kind of question. Hence one of his readers might, for the sheer pleasure of finding out, study Greek and Latin authors to see if they could throw more light on it. Such random curiosity certainly cannot be denied, and intellectual interest is just as human as economic interest. But the ideas which are its object are not in a world of their own but in this spatial world of change, multiplicity, and diversity.

It is fair to say, since we have brought in the ancients, that the idea of the prophetic power of omens was far commoner in the pagan period and that it could be said to be characteristic of it. But there were plenty of people who did not believe in omens, and Plutarch tells us of the ridicule that they expressed about them. In short, what I am saying is that there was not a pagan spirit which made men believe in omens, but that in the pagan period more people believed in them than do now. Yet even today superstition is not dead and there are always some dupes who will get ready for the end of the world on a determined date because, they say, it is predicted in the book of Revelation.

If I am willing to grant that it is appropriate to speak of a pagan period, what do I think determines its character? First of all, a pagan is an Occidental who is not a Christian. Therefore it is appropriate to speak of a period before Christianity was revealed. But when one gets down to details, one has to distinguish between the great mass of untrained men and women and the intellectuals. In the former group there was more or less variation. But the slaves, usually the women and the artisans, do not count when one is trying to find out what the spirit of Mediterranean antiquity was like. Second, when people speak of the Greeks, they usually mean the Athenians of the Periclean Age and the fourth century. But Greek literature runs from Homer, 9th century B.C., to at least the

sixth century A.D., though Byzantine literature continued
to be written much later. People speaking Greek and
writing Greek lived from lands near the Black Sea to the
Straits of Gibraltar. Up to very recently (if not now)
peasants in southern Italy used a Greek dialect in their
familiar talk. All these people, spread out over an area
with an axis of a thousand miles, had different ideas,
and the western pagans were aware of it. Nothing dis-
gusted the Roman literary critics so much as "oriental-
ism." But this was Greek, which was as obnoxious to, for
instance, Petronius as French phrases used to be to Trol-
lope or Thackeray. One hardly expects everyone who
speaks English to have the same ideas—Englishmen,
Australians, Canadians, Kentucky mountaineers, and
New Englanders. When writers speak of the Greek
mind, they forget that the New Testament exists only in
Greek, not in Aramaic, and that it is the Greek of the
common people. It is also forgotten that the Mass was
originally said in Greek and that to this day the opening
words, *Kyrie eleison*, are Greek. The variety of ideas
among Greek writers would be hard to catalogue. And
even that sweet reasonableness that some Hellenophiles
insist is the distinguishing mark of the Greek spirit was
certainly as foreign to Aristophanes and the writers of
the Old Comedy as it was to Euripides. I need not speak
of the prosecutors of Socrates. There was no Greek view
of life; there were various views of life held by Greeks.
No civilization can be summed up in a phrase.

Certain problems are fashionable at one time and go

out of style at another. The question of animal souls was a burning question in the latter part of the seventeenth century and now is just a subject for historians. The Battle of the Ancients and the Moderns, which blackened many a page of white paper at about the same time, now has been settled by exterminating the ancients. Again, few people today try to reconcile the first chapter of Genesis with what the geologists say, yet a hundred years ago this was a favorite pastime of some who had respect both for science and for the Bible. No one any longer argues about the superiority of masculine to feminine brains, but that too was a burning question even as late as 1920 or thereabouts. The nineteenth century did not get heated up over evolution because it was the nineteenth century or the Victorian Period; Darwinism was supposed to conflict with generally held religious dogmas and everybody at all times thinks of his religion as very precious, whether it be Buddhism, Christianity, Humanism, or Naturalism. Hardly anyone can get as excited over his religious ideas as an atheist. Analogous remarks could be made about each of the ideas I have mentioned. Descartes did not say that animals had no souls; he said, following Deuteronomy, that their souls are the blood. But people who had pets felt that their pets were closer to humanity than flesh and blood alone. The superiority of the ancients to the moderns involved the literary interests of men who were writing in an original way and wanted the right to do so. But there was a tradition that held that the older a thing was, the better. Primitive Christianity, primitive simplicity, our Founding Fathers, the ancient Romans, the Classics —all were terms carrying a heavy emotional charge. The discussion was muddied by the introduction of the thesis of eternal values and, clearly, modern literature could not embody them if it was unlike traditional literature.

Finally, it should be repeated that no idea exists in isolation from others except on paper. The people who demanded the right of the modern author to be appreciated on the same level as Homer or Vergil may not have been aware that they were also denying the theory of the eternal values, but it was because someone had denied it that his plea gained plausibility. This in turn was probably fortified by the success of the Protestant Reformation with its emphasis on freedom of conscience, a freedom that it did not grant to others. But it is also true that the invention of printing gave readier access to new ideas than had been possible before. The importance of this is seen in the establishment of licenses to print, of the censor, of the *Index Expurgatorius,* all of which looked as if the authorities were terrified lest the new ideas seem much more persuasive than the old. Heresies had been known long before printing was invented. When one examines them now in the cool light of detachment, with the exceptions of Arianism they do not seem very plausible. One wonders whether they would have gained any adherents if they had not been persecuted. Is it not an inherent trait of human beings to want to taste forbidden fruit?

The historian of anything whatsoever has to have a certain amount of simplicity and regularity. When people speak even of "human beings," they have already ironed out all the diversity and irregularity that men and women exhibit. When they speak of "adult males," they have already discarded a great many human beings in order to deal with a more homogeneous group. If they then go on to speak of "adult males, white," they have simplified still further, and before one knows, they have reached "white adult Protestant males with annual incomes between $8,000 and $15,000 in manufacturing towns of a population of over 25,000 owning their own houses and at least one car." Before long they will get down to John Smith.

One of the lessons a historian of ideas learns is that the intellectual milieu in which an idea is launched will influence its expression, that is, university professors talking about their specialty might be expected to qualify what they say more delicately than a writer for a popular magazine would. An idea as it seeps down into the less educated part of society becomes more and more vague and consequently less verifiable. It has often been pointed out that Russian polity is far from Marxism, and that is true if one means by Marxism only what was written in *Das Kapital.* But to the Russian, Marxism is what goes on in Russia at the time of speaking, and to the American, Marxism is a threat. Neither has probably read a word of Marx. To take another familiar example, Freudianism to a psychoanalyst is what Freud himself wrote.

To the average reader of the weekly press it is a lot of prurient talk about sex. But conversation is blocked if, when a man says something about an idea, his interlocutor immediately replies, "What do you mean by evolution?" "What do you mean by happiness?" "What do you mean by war?" And what would civilization be without conversation?

All historical—I do not say scientific—explanation is the fitting of a datum into a preconceived pattern which will include both the datum that is to be explained and all data that have already been explained. Hence when one sees an odd-looking painting hanging on the wall of a museum, the following types of explanation may be heard: (1) He (the artist) is just trying to show off; (2) He is expressing his emotions, not his perceptions; (3) A picture should not mean but *be* (*pace* MacLeish); (4) This is abstract expressionism, *or,* academic realism, *or,* post-impressionism; in other words it is an example of a named school of painting; (5) A typical Joe Dokes, i.e., it is what is to be expected from the particular man who painted it; (6) It just leaves me cold.

This can be extended *ad lib*. My point is that when something unusual seems to demand explanation, the only way one can explain it is by locating it among a larger class of objects. In the case I have cited, there is no science of aesthetic criticism in the sense that there is no generally accepted technique as there is in the sciences. But the fact that a physicist knows how to classify his data implies that he has already accepted a pattern in terms of which he will arrange them. He may be so used to his technique that it drops out of sight and consciousness. But that is quite a different matter from having no pattern. In the case of painting the same unconsciously applied pattern used to be representation, and the usual question that was asked of a painting which puzzled an onlooker was, "What is it a painting of?" But this question was no more necessary than a dozen others. Within reason, one can say that there are no schools of scientists. But there are schools of aesthetic criticism, of historiography, of theology, of psychology, and so on. There is a fundamental difference.

· 7 ·

The Personal Factor

If ideas are initiated by human beings, then the makeup of the individual may have something to do with the character of his ideas. This has been emphasized particularly since the early nineteenth century, but it is really nothing new. Plutarch in his life of Cicero says that Cicero was urged to forget the tastes of the public and follow the dictates of his own genius. So Polonius told his son to be true to himself as he left for Paris. And very much earlier Socrates was said to have an inner voice, the *daimon*, which restrained him from doing what he ought not to do. Neither the *daimon* nor the genius was what we mean by the self; they were authorities within the person and acting as guide. But exactly what are we driving at when we tell a man to be true to himself and not care what others think of him? What actually is this self? Is it simply the blank antecedent of the first personal pronoun serving as the subject of verbs? What is being expressed when we speak of self-expression? Of what are we conscious when we speak of self-consciousness? What is being satisfied in self-satisfaction? Or denied in self-denial? Is there a nuclear something in consciousness which "has" emotions, "does" the thinking, "feels" the feelings? Or is this self just a word that in reality denotes nothing? It is always important to square one's language with ordinary language if possible. And since we do speak of the "person's" contribution to the history of ideas, we might investigate what a person is.

When we ask these questions we enter a field that is even more obscure than most of those in which we have roamed. But let us hazard a guess, that when we speak of a person's self, we mean one or a combination of the following.

1. A person's way of thinking, the acuity of his intellect, his analytical power.

This is the kind of personality that we often attribute to lawyers and scientists, the ability to spot assumptions and see implications. This might be expressed in a man's ideas if, for instance, he was quick to detect a complex idea and break it down into its elementary parts. Such a man would never be content with discussing anything until it was analyzed. He would want crystal-clear definitions. Socrates seems to have had this type of personality, with one reservation: he was not dogmatic and he submitted all his definitions to examination. Regardless of that, one has but to read a lawyer's brief to recall how all evidence, all precedents, all the things that have to be proved, the *demonstranda*, are carefully set down and laid out in order.

The influence of such a man on the history of ideas would be like that of the late Professor A. O. Lovejoy. In his *The Great Chain of Being* he takes a simple sentence out of Plato's *Timaeus*[1] and shows how its supposed implications were worked out in subsequent history. To do this one has first to imagine the possible inferences, true and false, that might be drawn and then to see whether they actually had been drawn or not. And of course to imagine this is impossible without having first read an enormous amount of material which one suspects might have some bearing on the subject. To take an example of how one's imagination might suggest inferences that might be drawn from a simple idea, let us take the case of being true to oneself. Historically, not much extra reading is needed to know that one Greek, Socrates, believed that he had an inner guide, that the Romans believed that every man had his genius and every woman her Juno, who were not identical with the persons but who helped them, watched over them, and spoke to them through an inner voice. In Christianity the same function was performed by the guardian angels. They were different from their charges, just as geniuses

[1] The Demiurge "being devoid of envy, desired that everything should be so far as possible like himself, this then being above all the sovereign originating principle of Becoming and the cosmos."

were, and also helped their charges as geniuses did. The importance of this for our purposes is that we can see an idea held by a number of different people to the effect that a person contains within himself a voice that helps him in his decisions, usually moral. This inner voice might act in a variety of ways: like Socrates' *daimon* it might be a restraining influence, as our conscience is said to restrain us from doing something that is considered to be evil. It might be a source of divine illumination: Philo Judaeus receiving inspiration is a good example. It might be simply artistic inspiration.

In the beginning the emphasis is on its externality. Its words are not one's own. But the history of thinking shows a tendency to depersonalize forces, to accept them as they occur. One either speaks of them as something mysterious, an "I know not what," or simply records their action. The *thing* begins to give way to the *event*. Thus one begins to omit all reference to an agent outside oneself and to note either with wonder or with complacency what has happened. The guardian angels and attendant spirits give way to influences which are anonymous. But since there has to be an agent for every act, regardless of metaphysics, the acts of the spirit are referred to oneself. Then if one is highly intellectual, a good mathematician or logician, or highly artistic or religious, the intellectual, artistic, and religious interests are no longer put into one by an external agent but are one's own. It is now recognized that a human being is capable of making decisions without outside help. To be sure, this had been recognized in moral situations, for the will was reputed to be free to do whatever it chose. The self is now an intellectual self and its ideas are concerned with its intellectual interests.

2. But no one has yet been a pure intellect. The angels in St. Thomas Aquinas approached that condition as a limit, and the lowest rank, the Guardian Angels, could feel at least pity for their charges.

There are a number of things that we do without thought and these things are often attributed to instinct. We speak of a man of good and bad instincts, of instinctive cowards or instinctive heroes, of congenital misers or innate poets. No one today is quite sure how to explain the instincts of animals, let alone human beings, and the word is frowned upon in scientific circles. But the fact remains that most of us do not know why we are interested in, say, history or art or science; we simply know that a work of history captivates us and a work in chemistry leaves us cold; that when we see a picture, we want to stand before it and absorb it; that when we see a spider spinning its web, we want to watch and explain, if possible, why it behaves as it does, not simply to watch it as a spectacle. We may trace our interest back to a teacher whom we admired, but there were also others in his classes who were not influenced by him. Moreover, the fact that we admire a man does not imply that we would accept all his interests as our own. Whether these "instinctive" interests are congenital or not we do not know. But we can truthfully say that we have never seen a satisfactory explanation of them. We have heard of egocentric people, of altruistic people, of inner-directed and outer-directed people, but all such names are labels which are pinned on people after the fact and are not explanations. I mean by this that they do not tell us whether a person is determined from birth to be introverted or extraverted, to take one example, or whether he is free to be either and is influenced by other people and events in the direction he eventually takes ("eventually" being the age of eight or nine).

3. The personality of a man may also be defined by his emotions.

Some men give way to anger or pity very easily. They have, as they say, bad tempers or good tempers, and what angers one individual may arouse simply pity in another. Most of the "characters" in such books as those by Theophrastus or La Bruyère are defined by their habitual emotional reactions. They are braggarts, vainglorious, irate, cowardly, hypocritical. It is assumed that a man will have a character, and a character is nothing that he can control. It is caused by something that existed when he was born. Nowadays people talk of genes as determining character; a few years ago it was the endocrine glands; before that it was one's horoscope; and before that the humors. The theory of humors is not very different from the theory that the endocrine glands make us angry or gloomy or excitable or what not. The Greek Humoralists maintained that the body, every human body, was constituted by the blood, the phlegm, the

black bile, and the yellow bile. From the predominance
of one humor one became either sanguine, phlegmatic,
melancholy, or choleric—adjectives that we have retained, and have retained probably because they do
define types of emotional human beings better than
others. The sanguine person was generally happy, saw
the bright side of things, was therefore optimistic, and
all this because his blood was his predominant humor;
whereas the melancholy person, in whom the black bile
predominated, was of dark complexion, gloomy, and all
the other things that are listed by Burton in his *Anatomy
of Melancholy*. Just what "predominate" means is obscure, but then so are the humors themselves. Blood,
phlegm, and bile are realities, but they no longer have
the character that the Greek physicians gave them. Whatever the truth of temperaments or characters, they are
always defined by the emotional responses that people
give in their encounters with the world.

4. A fourth differentiating mark is found in the field
of perception.

Not only are some people more acute in one sense or
another than the run of humanity, but some seem to
be visually oriented, others auditorily, others toward
some one of the other senses. A visually minded person
will notice the visual aspect of things—their looks, their
colors, their shapes—and when he writes he will use
visual similes and metaphors. Vision has always been
thought of as the most important human sense, and
even the blind will use visual language to describe their

experiences. There are exceptions. I once heard a blind man say that, when he was waiting in a dentist's office, a woman came in "with a rustle of taffeta and the smell of heliotrope," none of which is visual and all of which is very vivid. Because of the importance of vision in the normal life, most people are trained to be visual to the exclusion of their other senses. But there are, nevertheless, people whose ears are very acute and who can identify a person by the sound of his voice. In fact the very blind man who gave me the description just noted identifies all his friends by their voices and speaks of young and old voices, tired and exuberant voices. Our other senses are dulled by lack of use, but there is no reason why we should not develop our sense of smell, for we are surrounded by potential olfactory experiences as well as by visual and auditory. Indeed, odors are often astonishing reminders of the past, as readers of Marcel Proust will recall.

If the self is the perceiver, then his ideas will be grounded in perceptual experiences. Oddly enough, this is exactly what happened in the seventeenth and eighteenth centuries in what was called "empirical" philosophy and psychology. According to this type of theory, all the "contents of the mind" were said to be compounds of sensory data, whether those alleged contents were perceptual or not. That is, even emotions and volitions and the belief in self-identity, as well as very complicated scientific ideas, were mosaics of which the tesserae were colors, sounds, odors, textures, and tastes. Experience thus conceived is not what the word usually denotes. One's disappointments, one's hopes, one's loves and hates, one's desires—these would not then be part of ones' experience. But the bare data of vision and the other sense organs are. Such a type of empirical philosophy clearly overlooked the amount of interpretation that is involved in a single declarative sentence. When one is asked, "What's that?" the answer, "A patch of red," is not anticipated except as sarcasm. What is expected is an answer like, "The communist flag," "An auction is going on," or "The Harvard Club."

5. One more item will suffice to show the complexity of the question of what the self is insofar as ideas are concerned. In society—and all men live in some society, in fact in several at one and the same time—a person is frequently identified by his descent.

He is, let us say, of either French birth or descended from French ancestors. He is of a highly rated social stratum or of one of the lower orders. His genealogy is distinguished or commonplace. And when a man is asked, "Who are you?" he may reply, "The eldest son of the fourteenth baron Nerdowell." Or he may reply, "I'm a Franco-American." The possibilities are very great. Those of us who are democratically inclined sometimes resent this sort of question, even when phrased less brusquely, for we feel that we are what we do and not what our ancestors were. For we can claim no credit for having ancestors greater than ourselves. Yet this assumption has had a real influence in the history of ideas, for it lies behind the whole theory of hereditary monarchy, of inherited property, of superior and inferior races and lineages, and none of these samples is trivial as far as human history is concerned. If I may again refer to Plutarch, to read him is to see how firmly embedded in that author's mind was the idea of superior and inferior blood. The ideas of men of superior rank are given wider extension than those of inferior rank and, furthermore, seem to have had more credibility. We all remember how this idea reigned among the Germans in the Nazi period, and the Germans had more university graduates than any other people in Europe. It is not a trivial matter if a man feels himself congenitally superior to others and if the others agree. One's imagination staggers at what has happened in the last 2,500 years because certain individuals had this idea and were able to convince others of its truth. Many a marriage has gone on the rocks because parents accepted its truth. Many a second-rate man has got a good job and many a first-rate man has failed to get one for the same reason. The dynastic principle extends well beyond politics—it accompanies in somewhat concealed form the whole idea of schools of thought in which disciples inherit their master's wisdom, and there is a sort of apostolic succession through spiritual fathers to their descendants. The blood here is imaginary, but the succession is thought of in terms of blood.

If what we have said is not too superficial, we can now raise the question whether personality is congenital or acquired. Recent investigations into molecular biology have led some of us to think that everything a person does is built into him at birth. For if our genes are complex molecules of DNA and our characters are in our genes, then there seems to be no escaping the conclusion that we are predetermined to be whatever we are. But surely a great deal of what we are is in our behavior, and there is no such behavior until after birth except for intrauterine kicks. But it may still be true that the way we react to external stimuli is predetermined. That is, one is not so much concerned with the color of one's hair or one's height or weight, though these too have some importance as we develop, but we are concerned with the manner in which we react to our fellow men, to our reading, to formal education. Much of this may be congenital in the sense that one is aggressive or submissive from birth, or quick or slow to react to perceptual stimuli, like light and sound. But those stimuli and others are not part of our heredity and vary from person to person. After all, parents, siblings, teachers, merchants, service employees surround us, and a good many of them are there to educate us, to change our spontaneous reactions for our supposed betterment or for the ease of social communication. Our parents, siblings, and teachers, to say nothing of clergymen and writers of edifying literature, all exist for the purpose of changing a child's personality, of making it either more conformable or less so. But none of these influences are in our DNA. This is being written during a presidential election campaign and the papers are black with recorded speeches of the candidates, who are trying either to make us change our minds or to resist all temptation to do so. What might be called education in the broadest sense of the word is what goes on throughout experience, which has been phrased as "learning from experience." If one does not or cannot learn from experience, then all schooling, all reading, all listening to lectures are futile. Do we just store up a great collection of facts in our memories or are our characters modified? The question is still moot, after how many tens of thousands of years of human society?

There does seem to be the possibility that people fall into certain more or less vaguely defined classes. This is based solely on my own teaching experience, not on a controlled experiment. Undergraduates, whatever may be true of others, seem to be either mathematically and scientifically minded or literary and artistic. These are two extremes, for there have been physicists who have been also artistic, witness Einstein, and at least one or two artists who were scientifically inclined, witness Leonardo. But as a rough generalization it holds. Yet it is based on personal impressions of university students who have already been subjected to about twenty years of experience. On the other hand, people do not indulge in the formulation of ideas to any appreciable extent until they are at least twenty, for day-dreaming must be counted out. At any rate, if people can be classified into types, it may be expected that the ideas which they entertain will be affected by their type. The importance of this comes out not when one is thinking of the origin of ideas but of the direction they will take once arisen. For one of the most curious facts about the history of ideas is the way they flow out of their original beds into the surrounding country. Thus, as we have indicated, evolution in the middle nineteenth century was usually thought of as a biological idea, but it took almost no time for it to over-flow into sociology, education, aesthetics, and even reli-gion. The value of the democratic process again might be thought of as essentially a political idea, but it has been applied as a test of artistic value, of ethical right-ness, and in Congregationalism in ecclesiastic organiza-tion. To say that a practice is undemocratic is to criticize it harshly even where democracy as a political system is not in question. At best a democratic decision is based upon more than 50 per cent of the people present and voting. The system has certainly worked better than any other in politics. But to imagine that over 50 per cent constitutes a measure of moral, aesthetic, religious, eco-nomic, or hygienic value is nonsense. The People know what they want at the moment of voting, but they have no more power of foretelling the outcome of their votes than 1 per cent of them do.

When the personal factor is accepted as a force in changing the course of intellectual history, then naturally the historian is faced with the problem, first, of a writer's sincerity and, second, of how far he is aware of what he is writing. No idea is any the less true because it was pronounced by a hypocrite, but that an idea has appealed to a hypocrite is of some historical significance. One of the best examples of how this raises a problem for the historian is the case of Pierre Bayle. Bayle has been charged with hypocrisy on the ground that after writing a long article showing what he believed to be the absurdity of some Christian belief, he then says that regardless of the absurdity we can and must believe it on faith, since the Church orders us to. There is some doubt about the sincerity of a man who would spend so much time pointing out the absurdity of ideas that he urges us to adopt. In Tertullian's case the situation is different, for he believed in a kind of reason that was "higher" than human reason, whatever "higher" means. When he said that he believed in the Incarnation because it was absurd, not in spite of its being absurd, he was claiming the right to believe in the occurrence of an individual unique historical event which, since it was unique and historical, was bound to be nonrational. People might also accuse Hume of insincerity when he argued against the reasonableness of the usual ideas of necessary causation and self-identity. On the other hand, he was simply carrying out the implications of his method. His opponents who accept the method and then refuse to accept its consequences are the ones who are insincere. If one's premises logically imply that the idea of a necessary cause is nonsensical, then one should give up the idea. But for reasons that are psychological and not logical at all, people wanted to retain the idea of a necessary cause as they did that of a permanent self. Hence they attacked Hume.

Those attacks (for some of which see Boswell's *Johnson*) were aimed at the wrong target, but they kept alive a set of ideas that were influential in the history of thought. It is questionable whether or not a historian should go into the matter of an author's sincerity, though it is worthwhile knowing whether or not he is ironical.

The second matter is of more importance. When an idea becomes so commonplace that people utilize it without recognizing it, then obviously it has triumphed. It has been welded into the ways of thinking of the most influential members of the Republic of Letters. I doubt very much that when literary critics praise a book for its unity or dispraise it for its lack of unity, they are at all aware of the history of the idea of unity. In philosophy alone, to say nothing of literary criticism, we find that for the earliest Greek philosophers, the Milesians, unity meant unity of matter. If they could show that all things were made of the same stuff, they would be satisfied. But then there was soon an emphasis on unity of structure by men like the Pythagoreans and on unity of formula or law in Heraclitus and dialectical unity by the Eleatics, a unity which must exist because they had proved to their own satisfaction that multiplicity was logically impossible. Unity became a eulogistic term and the variety of gods gave way to monotheism in which the multiplicity of polytheism gave way to the multiplicity of angels and saints and devils. There was unity of purpose, unity of method, unity of power, and so on. But if someone were to ask a critic why a unified book was better than a nonunified book, the critic would be amazed at the stupidity of the question.

No discussion of the biographical factor would be more than crudely superficial if it omitted the nonlogical influences on the formation of ideas. The pragmatic element goes hand in hand with wish-fulfillment. That the consequences for religion, politics, and ethics have been raised as an argument against ideas cannot be doubted. It is seldom that a person is frank enough or aware enough of his intellectual motivation to say outright, "This idea must be propagated because belief in it will be useful to me, or to the social group to which I belong, or to the state." On the contrary, he is more likely to say, "This idea must not be propagated because it is harmful to. . . ." In this way certain ideas are blocked in their possible progress. It is not that they may not be factually true. It is, first, because they are plausible enough to be accepted by the average man and, second, because they are harmful. (The order is not one of importance.) Thus, at the time of writing, any ideas derived from the writings of Karl Marx are believed by many people to be harmful to the United States, and a man who believes in them, and admits it, may find it hard to get a job in certain colleges and universities. But though Marx's idea of dialectical evolution may have been factually wrong, his analyses of economic conditions in England have never been proved to be a distortion of the facts. Certain details may have been wrong. But in any event the book by Engels, his collaborator, *On the Condition of the*

Working Class in England, has been admitted to be a true description of a way of life. People who believed in civil rights for all, black or white, have been shot in Mississippi. And atheists, though not abused in England or France, have a hard time of it in parts of the United States. Hence, if ideas which the powers find harmful are thus prevented from being read, their place in history will be obscure. No one to this day really knows what the Albigensians believed. Innocent III saw to it that they were exterminated. There is no way of finding out much of anything of the early heresies—Marcionism, Gnosticism, Manichaeism. We know something of them, for they are denounced in the pages of the orthodox. But like the Sophists in Greece, we know them only through what their enemies said of them.

Many ideas, because of an author's fancy, are propounded in literary forms which may modify them or make interpretation difficult. The Platonic dialogues are a perfect case of this, and Ph.D. candidates have a holiday trying to tell what Plato meant in the *Parmenides* or the *Theaetetus* or even the early works. Ideas which occur in plays are expressed by one of the *dramatis personae*; this is inevitable. But then the question arises of who speaks for the author. Does Hamlet express Shakespeare's ideas or his own? Did Shakespeare want to arouse sympathy for Shylock and was the speech (Act I,3) beginning,

> Signor Antonio, many a time and oft
> In the Rialto you have rated me
> About my money and my usances . . . ,

supposed to win pity for Shylock or ridicule? Or, since we are speaking of Shakespeare, in the sonnet (54),

> O, how much more doth beauty beauteous seem
> By that sweet ornament which truth doth give,

does this commit Shakespeare to the theory of realism? Or is it simply one of the poetic ornaments, one of those conceits that was fashionable at the time? The point of view of this book is that the historian of ideas need not worry about an author's sincerity, though a biographer of the author should do so. Ideas appear in many guises and the notion that beauty is enhanced by truth falls into the same tradition that Keats's urn expressed about three centuries later, one of the sources of which is Aristotle's *Poetics*.

The biographical factor, then, is mainly useful for throwing some light on why a person holds certain ideas. It also shows how an idea gains currency. And if there are psychological types with which typical ideas are correlated, and if in a period there is a predominant number of a given psychological type, then, of course, the appropriate ideas will circulate at that time.

PART TWO

· 8 ·

The People

There are some ideas that contain within themselves a cluster of other ideas, both normative and descriptive. Among these is the idea of *the People*, which occurs in such phrases as, "The voice of the People is the voice of God," "Government of the People, for the People, and by the People," "the fickle People." In this respect it resembles the ideas of Nature, of Unity, of Progress, of the Organic, of Creativity. But more than any of these similar ideas, it has become embodied in political and social action and hence has taken on overtones of more intensity than any of the ideas mentioned except that of Nature.

To begin with the descriptive complexities, the term in Greek, *demos*, from which our word "democracy" is derived, did not mean all the residents of a Greek city-state. It meant a political district and only the citizens of that district. But these citizens were free-born Greeks who could theoretically trace their ancestry back to some mythical founder of their clan. The Greek cities, like medieval and modern societies, were socially stratified. According to Solon's laws, the people of Athens were divided into four classes based on the amount of property they owned. The richest class were alone eligible to the archonship and to all commands; the next richest were knights, having enough money to keep a horse and fight in the cavalry; the third class formed the heavy infantry and were bound to serve in full panoply; the fourth, or poorest, class were ineligible for any office of dignity, served in war in the light-armed infantry, were free from the income tax but had the right to elect the archons, and formed the public assembly which could call the archons to account for their management of public affairs. It would be difficult to decide who were the People in such a society. If in the United States only millionaires were eligible for the Presidency; men of fortunes between a million and five hundred thousand were eligible for the Senate and other federal positions of honor, such as posts in the Cabinet or on the Supreme Court; men with annual incomes of between $10,000 and $15,000 were alone eligible for election to Congress and the state legislatures; and the citizens who pay no income tax because of their poverty could vote but hold no offices whatsoever, one might have an analogous situation. In Athens there were the further restrictions that neither women nor resident aliens nor, needless to say, slaves formed part of the People in the political sense of that term.

In Sparta there were similar divisions, and also in Rome. The lowest class in Sparta, the Helots, had no rights and no political position, but, like the Plebeians in Rome, revolted from time to time, a technique of social action that was to be repeated throughout the history of Europe. The story of popular uprisings in Europe as a whole has yet to be told in detail but it is fair to say that the upper classes were seldom without the menace of rebellion from below. The curious thing about these rebellions is that none of them produced significant political or social changes until the nineteenth century.

In Rome the term *populus*, from which we get our word "people," was first distinguished from the Senate, a group of elders who were in theory descended from the Ramnes, who had been chosen by Romulus. But the word also meant all the people of Rome. At the same time it was occasionally distinguished from the plebeians and the adjective *plebeian* took on a pejorative connotation as it does in modern English. Sometimes a Roman would use the word *vulgus*, from which we get "vulgar," as a term of dispraise and it was probably synonymous with *plebs*. But there was a further complication when one spoke of "a" people, the Roman people (the English people, the American people), for in this usage all distinction of class was eliminated as well as all overtones of praise or dispraise. A people is a group of human beings, including women and children, who are united by sharing a common culture or, to use a criterion of Cicero's, by agreeing to observe the same laws, or, as in St. Augustine, by sharing a common religion. Thus "the Roman people" became all Romans, whether plebeians or patricians, whether rich or poor. And "thy people Israel (*tua plebs Israel*) became all Jews and Christians.

The political distinction between the People and others has an interesting history in the proverb, V*ox populi, vox Dei.* When the Jews came to Samuel and asked for a king, Samuel hesitated, knowing what a disaster kingship would turn out to be. He consulted the Lord, who said to him, "Listen to the voice of the people" (*Audi vocem populi* in the Vulgate). The voice of the People in this case was wrong and God knew that it was wrong. It was in all probability the voice of the Elders, not of all the people, all the inhabitants of the land of Israel. Similarly, when the authors of the Constitution of the United States opened that document with the words, "We, the people of the United States," the denotation of "people" was very narrow, as Professor Morris D. Forkosch has recently shown.[1] The men who wrote the Constitution represented twelve of the thirteen states and their opinions were far from being identical with those of their peers throughout the land. The debates in the Federal Convention show how diverse were the ideas even of those present and voting. In fact, in one sense of

[1] See his article, "Who Are the 'People' in the Preamble to the Constitution?" *Case Western Reserve Law Review,* xix, No. 3 (April, 1968), 644-712.

the word "people," the authors of the Constitution were afraid of "the People" and wanted to set up a government in which all the people would not be the ruling power. The word "democracy" was a bad word. It connoted mob rule, the rule of the *mobile vulgus*. And when the French Revolution broke out and the Terror got under way, the word "republic" was in worse repute. One has but to read the conditions for the franchise in the various states to see how suspicious the men of the federal period were of government by "all the people."

As history moves on we find that "the People" are among the following:

1. The governed as opposed to those who govern, whether king, senate, or parliament. Even when the word has no unpleasant connotations, and when a government is said to be representative of the wishes of all the people, still a distinction has to be made between the governors and the governed. This is true even in the United States Constitution. The Ninth Amendment, for instance, reads in part, "The enumeration of certain rights shall not be construed to deny or disparage others retained by the people," and the Tenth similarly says, "The powers not delegated to the United States by the Constitution, nor prohibited by it to the States, are reserved to the States respectively, or to the people." The People here are clearly not the government, either federal or state. It is a question that has yet to be decided just what these rights are and just who the people are who possess them. But the verbal distinction is obvious.

2. In certain writers, the People are the peasants who

are supposed to be "closer to the soil" than large landowners and urban dwellers. For Michelet, the People
were only the peasants and the rest of the population
were nonpeople. It is likely that in his book *Le Peuple*,
Michelet had in the back of his mind that a People was
properly only the descendants of the purest French
lineage, those whose ancestors had mated only with individuals of similar stock, whereas in the city all sorts of
alien blood had mingled with the French. Similarly in
Wordsworth's preface to the *Lyrical Ballads*, the People
are again the peasants, for they are the residue of the
purest English stock and speak the purest English.

3. In contrast to this, some writers, Chancellor Kent
for instance, thought that only landowners were the
People and alone should have any say in the government.
It is reported that John Jay had said, "Those who own
the country should rule it." Whether he did or not, the
property qualifications for the franchise which persisted
in many of the states for many years indicate that his reported opinion was shared in deed if not in words. The
country in this context was the land, but it did not take
many generations for Americans to learn that one did
not need to own land to own a good share of the country. For as manufacturing took over from agriculture and
the overwhelming portion of the population moved to
cities, ownership of land became irrelevant to political
power.

4. A modern distinction is made between the People
as "the Workers" and those who control management,

capital, "the Establishment." The new "People's Democratic Republics" are supposed to be governed by the working class whether urban or rural. In the French Revolution when Robespierre spoke of the People, he referred to artisans, small shopkeepers, hack writers, *le menu peuple*, and not the middle class.

5. There has also been made a distinction between the "true" people and, presumably, the false. In Hitler's opinion only men and women who had no detectable trace of Jewish, and probably no Negro or Slavic, blood were the true German people. The possession of one "non-Aryan" grandparent was enough to disqualify one, though a few individuals were honorary Aryans. This was not dissimilar to the distinction made by the Spartans between Spartans and Helots along with the *perioikoi*, provincials who were free but not citizens of Sparta. The Helot was probably not of the same blood as the true Spartan. If the caste system in India was originally based on racial decent, it would be another example of the distinction between a true and a false people. The descendants of the Dravidians would in that case not be true Indians.

6. We next have to list a distinction which is purely social and distinguishes between those who are high in the hierarchy of social prestige—either the rich, or descendants of old families, or landed gentry, or men and women of fame or notoriety (the distinctions sometimes overlap)—and those who are of the lower classes, the poor, newcomers to the community, in the United States

immigrants or their children, people who rent their houses instead of owning them, the great masses of the relatively unknown. When one hears the phrase "the people of the United States," or "the American people," one does not know which group is being referred to. It depends upon who is speaking. As I shall try to show, either group may be thought of in a eulogistic way or the opposite.

7. In aesthetic matters the People become the Folk. The Folk above all must not have had much schooling. Their arts must be traditional or close to it. The auto-didact painter, the peasant singer, the Negro jazz player, persons who practice some art but are not of the Academy, qualify as the People here. Folk dances, folk art, folk song, along with the canvases of the "Sunday painters," become more representative of the People than works of art made by trained artists.

Each of these meanings of the People has affective coefficients, both pleasant and unpleasant. What is vulgar is dispraised, but when the word "folk" is used in place of "vulgar" the same thing is praised. Socially the lower classes are not thought worthy of associating with the upper classes, but sometimes their language and their manners are affected by the latter. At the time of writing, the vocabulary of the slums has become stylish and ladies and gentlemen use the obscene and scatalogical vocabulary of their supposed inferiors with the greatest indifference. This may be a symptom of egalitarianism, but it is probably rather that *nostalgie de la boue* which all of us suffer from at certain moments. Thus the demotic, the popular, the plebeian takes on a racy quality of which a person may be proud if it is not innate in him but acquired. The rough diamond is usually unconscious of how rough he is, but the man who affects the manners of the rough diamond is well aware of his pose. The nostalgia for the gutter is not a weakness of those born to it.

It seems unlikely that anyone living in classical Athens or Augustan Rome or at the court of the great Duke of Burgundy would have deliberately acted like a peasant or an artisan. The proletariat was usually represented in literature and art as comic, loutish, ignorant, crude, and sometimes lazy, only very rarely as pitiable. Plautus represents the fishermen of *Rudens* as pitiable to modern eyes, but one does not know how they struck the Romans who saw them and heard them. After all there are people even in this humanitarian age who think the *Taming of the Shrew* is funny. Our ancestors were much more heartless than we realize and a history of what was believed to be comic would prove very enlightening. When the peasants or plebeians revolted, and they revolted frequently, they were put down without mercy. The serf had some rights but so few that they were to the modern mind trivial. It would be unthinkable in the United States to pass a law forbidding sharecroppers to send their sons to school, especially if they were white men. Yet a similar law was passed in the England of Edward III, with a difference that the sharecroppers were serfs. A good idea of how the common people were thought of

in the time of Shakespeare comes out in *Julius Caesar*—
"you sticks, you stones, you worse than senseless things."
But that was still a period in which rank conferred privileges and one's dignity was rewarded with special rights.
The social hierarchy then was still a real hierarchy, and
a man was supposed to know and remain in his place.

A hierarchy of social prestige has always and everywhere existed, as far as the records show, and this applies
even to the so-called primitive societies. Lloyd Warner
and Paul S. Lunt in *The Social Life of a Modern Community* have distinguished six classes in a typical American town and have found that language, place of
residence, religion, lineage, clubs, types of entertainment
and sports vary from class to class. In some details,
lineage for instance, the lower lower-class will resemble
the upper upper-class, but their members will vary in
their occupations, religious affiliations, places of residence, and so on. In England and in France, and possibly
in the other European countries, there are still residues
of the official social hierarchy in the distinction between
the various levels of nobility and the commoners. And
though the nobility in France has no legal status whatsoever, titles are retained and used and, as all readers of
Marcel Proust are aware, the nobles form a closed social
group and even live in or around the same quarter, the
Quartier Saint-Germain. Few Englishmen or Frenchmen
take this status seriously, but at least in England the
novels emphasize the social origin of their characters to
an extent that would be unheard of in the United States.

The People

To be a gentleman on one side of the Atlantic means to behave in a certain way; on the other side it means rank. The consciousness of class comes out very clearly in the novels of C. P. Snow, though it emerges of course in every novelist from Fanny Burney on.

The People in such a context may be either the members of the upper strata or of the lower, depending on whether the word is used eulogistically or not. In the United States the economic hierarchy probably counts for more than the social, for social mobility is very quick here. Multimillionaires, millionaires, the well-to-do, the comfortably well off, the poor—all represent distinctions that have importance. The power of money is and always has been very great in acquiring privileges, but nowhere has it been accompanied by such admiration as in America. We all ridicule the *nouveaux riches*, but whether riches are new or old is a small matter in the eyes of the public at large. In fact, if they were acquired by a self-made man, that is all to his credit, whatever his manners, his morals, or his social conscience. Someone, a Sinclair Lewis, might introduce a modern Trimalchio, but most writers no longer deal with the rich, whether new or old. It is presumably no longer good form to lay one's plots in drawing rooms. And indeed it must be confessed that the ladies and gentlemen of, for instance, Henry James do seem a bit quaint today, however much we may admire their creator's linguistic subtleties. In the economic hierarchy the People are those who are controlled by the rich, the power of whom may be exercised in occult ways. The Lobbies, for instance, represent money and yet have been known to squelch proposed legislation as well as to write bills which are then voted on. They become a fourth power in the government.

Up to the Industrial Revolution the words "vulgar," "popular," and "plebeian" were terms of dispraise. They remain so in those circles which maintain linguistic tradition. We substitute for them "folk," and we retain "popular" as a term of praise. The lower classes, in whatever sense their rank is determined, are not generally despised or thought of as comic or made to look comic, for they have acquired all the political rights that the governing classes used to have. Political egalitarianism is accompanied by general egalitarianism. Distinctions and rewards based on social or economic rank are no longer accepted by the public with equanimity. What historical reasons can be given for this?

First, it should be noted that the shift in opinion began with pity for the downtrodden. Charity in the sense of alms was a duty in both Jewish and Christian circles and there was plenty of reason given in both Testaments for helping the poor and the sick. But other than through alms little was done to prevent poverty and public ill health. The peasants in post-Pagan Europe began to revolt with the Bagaudae in at least the third century, yet their leaders evoked little sympathy from the ruling classes. Similar remarks might be made about Lollardry in England; the very name became a term of abuse. The Chartist movement later on did cause some writers, Mrs. Gaskell and Charles Kingsley for instance, to write about the working man with sympathy. But what won him political power was the recognition on the part of management that if the workers refused to work, the mills would make no money. The Labor Movement gained power through organization, not through kindliness. This consolidated power did not create friendly feelings for the working class: the upper classes in the United States still do not regard the unions with affection. What techniques of rationalization were used to give the People, the *menu peuple*, the small farmer and the workingman, respectability?

First, there was undoubtedly the religious tradition of Judaism and Christianity, fortified by Roman Stoicism, which proclaimed all men to be brothers and fellow citizens, either in the City of God or in the Cosmopolis. Along with this there was in Stoicism the notion of the general consensus, the *consensus gentium*, as the test of truth: what all men believed must be true. This was utilized to justify the belief in proverbial philosophy as late at least as the middle nineteenth century. It is referred to by politicians when they say they are subservient to the public's will. But common sense, which entered technical philosophy with Thomas Reid, in order to be really common has to traverse social and economic, to say nothing of racial, lines.

Common sense was the voice of nature speaking. And nature manifested itself most clearly in those who were untouched by the artifices of civilization. Thus the peas-

ant living in the country and on the land, the workingman living on a small income were both able to get along
without luxuries, like the noble savage. They were more
natural than the princes and magnates. They followed
instinct, not learning; they were poets born and not
made; artists whose eyes were innocent like those of
children. Like the Greek Cynic or the Christian monk or
the Essene, they were able to get along with a minimum
of comfort, demanding nothing more than a bare living.
When the appeal to nature as norm was made, such men
could be held up as examples of naturalness.

But there was also the curious idea that the peasant
was of older stock than the city dweller. The antiquity of
one's blood was held in reverence and was sought as a
test of authenticity. The idea was applied in two ways,
ways that were not entirely reconcilable. For there were
always the nobles who could trace their lineage back further than the average commoner could do. In Greece
such men went back to some god or demigod, in Rome
to the companions of Aeneas, in Europe to one of the
Trojans or one of the descendants of the sons of Noah.
If a genealogy of such antiquity was not realizable, it
sufficed to go back to the companions of William the
Conqueror or to Charlemagne's paladins. Such men
were somehow closer to the source of the nation and thus
"true" Greeks, Romans, Frenchmen, Englishmen. On
the other extreme, the peasant, who had always apparently lived where he was, had been there from the founding of the nation. Michelet made a great deal of this.

The peasant was wedded to the soil of France and had always owned his *lopin de terre.* Michelet must have known that this was largely fiction, but that was of no importance. The peasant was especially antique, if one could believe that he had been on his land since it was first settled. And in most cases it was difficult to disprove this.

The People-as-Peasant lost their loutish character when urban agglomerations became disagreeable. The countryman who stayed on the land was in the minority and could be admired for sticking to his place, speaking his rustic dialect in a manner that no longer seemed comic. One sees the shift beginning in Thomas Hardy, where some peasants are treated in a patronizing manner —the rural choirs for instance—but where on the whole they are treated with respect. The English peasant now has a heart of oak. But once he goes to the city to work in the mills, he degenerates. Urban slums are not nurseries of good speech, obsequious manners, deference to higher social rank, or resignation above all. On the contrary, the person who grows up in the slums takes on an accent of vulgarity that to the ears of most upper-class people is revolting, and when he himself emerges into the comfortable life of the middle class, he tries to change his speech and manners. But when the social conscience of the upper classes was stirred by the misery of the slums, stirred probably more by the novelists than by any spontaneous burst of compassion, and when the economists pointed out that charity was not a solution to the problem, when the trade unions got under way and succeeded in improving the lot of the urban worker, then a revaluation of him and his fellows began. The extension of the franchise and the abolition of the property criterion gave the People, in the sense of the workingmen, more political power. To induce that power it was necessary in all probability that a new emotional attitude toward labor be aroused. The job was done by propagandizing for the "dignity of labor," to replace the more ancient idea that labor was a punishment inflicted on the human race because of Adam's fall.

The denotation of the People as far as the political context is involved has been extended to include all adult citizens in most places, whether naturalized or native born. Indeed, the denotation of "adult" has also been extended in some of the states to include people eighteen years of age. And it is all these men and women who are now the People. Whether they are urban or rural is of no importance, and in fact even the term "folk song" has been widened to cover the songs made by urban singers like Pete Seeger, Bob Dylan, Joan Baez, who a few years ago would not have been thought of as part of the Folk. Apparently what is demanded, when one praises the People for either their intelligence or their artistic ability, is the sense that the individuals concerned have merged themselves into some larger group, either by expressing themselves as the "average" human being does or by expressing themselves so as to please the average taste. It was believed in the eighteenth century that the folk songs were actually composed by the collective mind or spirit or soul of the Folk, not by an individual. That idea has been discarded. But at the same time there seems to be a feeling that some works of art, whether paintings or poems or songs, are more "popular" than others, not necessarily in the sense that they are liked by more people but in the sense that they express a popular spirit or soul.

If everybody is part of the People politically, the same cannot be said in other contexts. Society is still stratified and there are upper and lower classes. Literature is also stratified: there is the literature that is addressed to the Happy Few—to the highly sophisticated, to the cynical, perhaps to the scholars—books with a very restricted subject matter; at the other extreme are the comic strips and the movie magazines. No one, as far as I know, has ever classed Henry James with Frances Parkinson Keyes. The same is true of the visual arts: one does not think of Albers or Rothko as artists of and for the People; Norman Rockwell fills the bill more suitably. Andrew Wyeth would turn out to be on both ends at once. He is extremely popular, liked by large numbers of people, and he possesses a technique that if applied to less familiar subject matters than his—or to no subject matter at all —would be highly esteemed by the aesthetic elite. All this reduces to the question of the stratification of tastes and standards of behavior. And whether one lives in a democracy or in an absolute monarchy, one will discover the same phenomenon.

Hence the extension of the political denotation of the People is not accompanied by an extension of the ethical and aesthetic denotation. At the present time (1968) there is a widespread rebellion on the part of the young against the values and standards of tradition, whether those standards measure beauty or goodness. This rebellion is not confined to the United States or to continental Europe; it appears to be worldwide. It arises out of disgust with the hypocrisy of traditional society accompanied by outrage at the inequalities attached to racial and economic conditions. It is often expressed in the vocabulary of individualism, but people lose their individuality when they fight in the ranks. Hence these people have taken on a uniform which marks them as a group. They are obligated to conform to a group code, as any member of the capitalistic bourgeoisie is obligated. In respect of their program they are against the People; they form a People within the People. But they are not unique in this. In William Domhoff's *Who Rules America?* is outlined another group which is welded together by money, social prestige, education, even religion. And one can think of the other highly organized groups in the United States that wield power in more or less widely extended areas, areas which they have selected as their fields of action. The Latter-day Saints are by no means merely a religious group; the Movie and Television Magnates are not merely an aesthetic group; and the CIO-AFL is not merely a large trade union. The society of the United States is indeed a collection of such groups, and one suspects that the same is true of other countries.

The People

In short, the idea of the People today applies strictly only to those who, in the words of Professor Forkosch, are "citizens born or naturalized here and subject to the jurisdiction of [this country]." This is a purely political definition and covers almost everyone. As far as the United States as a whole is concerned, there is no other People; there are simply groups, societies, clubs, organizations for and against this and that. But where everyone is part of the People, the term has lost its selective power. The history of this idea, if I am right, is one of steady restriction. Whereas Cicero could try to work out an applicable definition of *populus* which would include those whom he wanted included and exclude those whom he wanted excluded, we are no longer faced with that problem. The word and its derivatives will continue to be used, but its primary meaning will be the political meaning and no value will be associated with it. The People will be the name simply for that group entitled to vote in elections for public office. They will be thought of as neither better morally nor more gifted aesthetically than anyone else—if there is anyone else to be compared to them. Popular music will be praised by some and dispraised by others, just as popular art always has been, and there will be disputes over its value. But that is to be expected, for tradition does not die quickly.

Since wealth and education will be unequally shared for some years to come, distinctions in society based on them will continue to subsist. It is unlikely that even if wealth were more equally divided tastes would be unified. It is also unlikely that ethical standards would become uniform, for even within a religious group, some people are good and some bad. There is dissension in the Earthly Paradise of the Communist countries, just as there is in primitive societies. Until all men are born with precisely the same genes and live in precisely the same environment there will be more or less difference of behavior. But no two people can live in the same environment for the simple reason that A is part of the environment of B, and B is part of A's. Historians of ideas will always have plenty of work to do.

·9·

Monotheism

Monotheism is of special interest to historians of ideas for two reasons. First, its history illustrates how a relatively simple idea can be retained over the centuries and change its meaning radically. Second, it is an idea in which most Occidentals believe in one form or another. Jews, Christians, and Muslims are monotheists and so are some rationalists deriving from eighteenth-century Deists. The latter group have thrown off the biblical account of God's nature but nevertheless believe in a God whose nature is discovered by metaphysical argument. A Deist may not be a Christian but he will insist that he believes in one God. And to complicate matters still more, there are clergymen who have proclaimed that God is dead but have retained belief in some being or other who has taken over His functions or some of them.

187

It would, moreover, be granted by most people in our culture that it is better to believe in one God than in many, that the development of monotheism among the ancient Hebrews conferred a blessing on western Europe, and that the polytheism of the Mediterranean pagans was an inferior kind of religious belief. The metaphysical pathos of the word "one" is very intense and should be studied by itself. In this sketch we shall take that for granted.

In what follows I have relied for the early beliefs of the Hebrews on Professor W. F. Albright's admirable *From the Stone Age to Christianity*, for the history related in it is based on expert knowledge not only of several ancient languages of which I am ignorant, but also of archaeology, of which my ignorance is as great. What follows that portion of this sketch is my own.

According to Professor Albright the earliest theology of the Hebrews was polytheistic. The principal deity was a mountain god, a member of the clan. Early South Arabian pantheons were often organized in triads of father, mother, and son, a system which is proto-Semitic. In primitive Hebrew religion the father was named El, the mother's name was obscure but perhaps Elat or Anath, and the son was a storm god, probably Shaddai, "the One of the Mountain(s)." Monotheism was introduced by Moses and God was given a name which must never be spoken, symbolized in the Tetragrammaton, a group of four letters which used to be spelled Jehovah but at present is transliterated Yahweh. In Exodus 3:14, this God says to Moses, "I am what I am," the most suitable sense of which is, according to Professor Albright, "He causes to be," which is equivalent to "He causes to be what comes into existence." He is thus essentially a creator. Not only is He a creator, but He is the creator of all things. He is, moreover, alone, having no family, without any special abode, is anthropomorphic but aniconic, no representation of Him being possible. Each of these characteristics, we might add on our own account, gave rise to certain problems and dogmas. If God was a creator, there must have been a period—no matter how defined—when there was nothing in existence. In the Middle Ages a distinction was made between creation, which was making something out of nothing (*ex nihilo*), and production, which was organizing or giving form to pre-existing matter. But when the scientific rule was laid down that nothing could come from nothing, a strong conflict arose between religion and science. In the second place, if He created all things, then He must have created evil as well as good, or else some other explanation must be given for the existence of evil. Some religions maintained that there was a god of evil as well as a god of good, and that there was conflict between them. But this type of belief was exterminated in the West, though the Prince of Darkness, Satan, was retained. In the third place, if He has no special abode, the belief in particularly holy places is eliminated and God will be said to be everywhere. How then is He to be distinguished from His creation? Unrestricted in territory,

He can be thought of as the universal God, not a local or tribal god—and the way was open for breaking down the religious barriers of the pagans with their gods on Mount Olympus. That God was anthropomorphic gave rise to the problem of how He resembled man. For man was made in His image and likeness, but the Decalogue as promulgated by Moses forbade the making of images. No image was possible, though many were made. Yet this did not obviate the problem of our resemblance to Him. It could hardly be anatomical, and a philosopher like Philo Judaeus ridicules all thought of God as having arms and legs, though "He walked in the Garden." The resemblance might then reside in the soul or in some part of the soul, or again the very idea of resemblance might be allegorical. Enough anthropomorphism might be retained to permit one to pray to Him and have a chance of being heard. But there were also many biblical verses speaking of His mercy, His anger, His love for His children, to induce a retention of many human traits. All of this gave rise, as we have suggested, to problems, most of which remain unsolved after three millennia and are still being debated.

Professor Albright points out possible Egyptian influences on the Mosaic idea of God, but these need not concern us. We begin our history with the Mosaic God, a god who is a creator, a source of justice, with ubiquitous power, and, though invisible and aniconic, yet anthropomorphic. As a source of justice, He became the supreme lawgiver, and the laws of the Decalogue, of Leviticus, and of Deuteronomy were thought of as revealed from the divine source. This gave Him a double function, that of a moral lawgiver, and that of a director of nature. The laws of physics and chemistry and all the other natural sciences emanated from Him, for there was no other divinity to proclaim them and they could not be satisfactorily explained as man-made. It requires no long meditation to see that such an idea would raise problems that would demand solution, that would need clarification, that would produce contradictions on the part of nonbelievers, which, consequently, would necessitate defense.

Meanwhile in Greece there developed the very antithesis of this kind of god. The Greek gods were localized, sometimes even in name. Thus, to take one example, there were the Ephesian Artemis and the Artemis of Brauron, the Artemis of Aegina and the Artemis of the Tauric Chersonese, all of whom probably began their careers as local divinities later merged into one; for the movement in classical antiquity was toward syncretism. We find, for instance, Kronos merged with Saturn and with Moloch of Carthage, Saturn a beneficent god and Moloch a bloodthirsty monster. At the same time a host of minor divinities developed out of abstractions like Faith and Hope and Victory, and this grew to such a point that it was ridiculed by Cicero in his work *On the Nature of the Gods*. All these gods were anthropomorphic and there was no taboo against representing them as beautiful superhuman beings. Their functions were limited, some of them taking special care of childbirth or disease, others of warfare or household duties or agriculture or the vine. In this they resembled some of the saints of Catholicism who are the patrons of carpenters, of sailors, of seamstresses, of goldsmiths. Their behavior was often far from moral and a man like Lucian did not hesitate to poke fun at them. Finally even Zeus himself, Father of gods and men, was not omnipotent: he was bound by the laws of Fate.

The Greek philosophers saw things differently. Xenophanes in the late sixth century B.C. saw clearly the absurdities of the popular myths. "Homer and Hesiod," he said,

> have ascribed to the gods all things that are a shame and a disgrace among mortals, stealings and adulteries and deceivings of one another. . . . Mortals deem that the gods are begotten as they are, and have clothes like theirs, and voice and form. Yes, and if oxen and horses or lions had hands, and could paint with their hands, and produce works of art as men do, horses would paint the forms of the gods like horses, and oxen like oxen, and make their bodies in the image of their several kinds. The Ethiopians make their gods black and snub-nosed; the Thracians say their gods have blue eyes and red hair. . . . [But there is only] one god, the greatest among gods and men, neither like unto mortals in form nor in thought. . . . He sees all over, thinks all over, and hears all over. . . . Without toil he swayeth all things by the thought of his mind. And he abideth ever in the selfsame place, moving not at all; nor doth it befit him to go about now hither now thither.[1]

[1] I use the translation of John Burnet in his *Early Greek Philosophy*, 3d ed., London, 1920, pp. 119f.

The unity of this deity did not prevent the existence of other deities; but it reduced them to a position of inferiority. The "one god" of Xenophanes resembles the Hebraic God in that he, too, is aniconic and omnipresent and, one gathers, unchanging. Nothing is said in the remaining fragments about his being the source of law, moral and physical, or whether or not he was to be worshiped. The fragments are too small to give us much evidence of their implications, but it is clear that they come from an attack on legendary mythology and in that respect resemble some of the exhortations of the Hebrew prophets.

A second example of philosophic theology is Cleanthes' *Hymn to Zeus.*

Most glorious of immortals, you of many names, ever omnipotent,
Zeus, ruler of nature, governing all by law,
Hail! for it is man's duty to address himself to you,
For we are your children, being, as it chances, the sole image of one,
Whatsoever mortals live and move about the earth,
Wherefore to you shall I sing hymns and your power shall I forever celebrate.
You and none other does the cosmos, circling round this earth, obey
Whithersoever you lead, and willingly is it led by you.
These have you as servants in your invincible hands,
The forked lightning, fiery, everliving;
When it strikes, all nature trembles.
By it you guide the universal *Logos*, which pervades all things,
Mingling with both the greater and the lesser stars;

As you have been and are supreme ruler of them all.
Nor is any deed done on earth against your will, O Lord,
Either in the high and divine heaven or on the sea,
Save that which evilmongers do in their madness.
But you know how also to render the even odd,
And to bring order into the unordered, and the displeasing is
    pleasing in your sight.
For so have you brought all things into unity, good with evil,
That the universal *Logos*, ever-being, has become one.
When the evil flee from it, they become
Miserable, and those of good men who always yearn for the
    possession of wealth
Neither see the common law of God nor listen to it;
But evildoers again and again strive indecently for something
    else,
Some possessed by passionate zeal for fame,
Some turned to craftiness in complete disorder,
And other to the shameless and voluptuous deeds of the
    body,
Hastening in all ways to become the opposite of the good.
But Zeus, giver of all gifts, shrouded with dark clouds, you of
    the bright lightning,
Free men from endless misery,
Which you, Father, may expel from their souls, and give us
    the power
To be governed by your mind, trusting in which you govern
    all things with justice,
To the end that honoring you, we may share in your honor,
Hymning your works continually, as it is fitting
For a mortal, since there is no better prize for men
Or for gods, than ever to celebrate the universal law in
    justice.[2]

[2] Stobaeus, *Eclogue Phys.* I, 12.

194

The Zeus of Cleanthes is above all a mind. He lays
down the laws for the cosmos and for men. He is a father
and may properly be addressed by his children in prayer.
His laws are rational, for the meaning of *Logos* is reason.
Yet there are evildoers on this earth who are irrational
and seek the wrong ends. He has not prevented their
existence but he does have the power to expel their evil
desires from them. There is very little here to differ-
entiate him from the biblical God of the prophets. However, certain notable omissions should not be passed
over. Nothing is said of his punishing mankind, as God
did in the Flood, nor of his anger, nor of sacrifice, nor
of miracles. Whether in other passages or in the works of
some other early Stoic such things were said, we have no
way of knowing.

In later Stoicism, Zeus becomes the ruler of the world-
city, the Cosmopolis, which in St. Augustine became the
City of God. All men are citizens of that City over which
Zeus rules, but in order to be good citizens, they must
follow reason, the *Logos*, which makes no distinction
between Greek and Barbarian, free man or slave. Marcus
Aurelius the emperor and Epictetus the slave were
brothers in the Cosmopolis.

Monotheism in classical antiquity came from the
philosophers who could not bring themselves to believe
in the absurdities of theological folklore. Similarly, in
Christian times there existed alongside the theology of
the philosophers a mass of superstition about weeping
statues, miraculous images, amulets, and the like. This

contrast between popular and philosophic religion, or theology, is one which has kept theological speculation alive. Thus far we have cited fragments of works to illustrate Greek monotheism. Plato, whose works exist in bulk, was the most important contributor to a mono-theistic theology among the pagans. His *Timaeus* in a Latin version was the philosophic Bible of the early Middle Ages. *Timaeus* is an account of how the Demiurge organized the world of matter. In spite of important differences between him and God, Plato's account of him was used as if those differences did not exist.

The Demiurge was timeless and unchanging like God, but purely rational, like Cleanthes' Zeus. Being rational and impassive, he had no love for human beings, nor any dislike of them. He was not interested in the passions of men. He formed men, as God did, but after their formation he seems to have had no further interest in them. His interests were in the cosmos as a whole. The Demiurge, moreover, was not a creator *ex nihilo*. Plato apparently could not conceive of making something out of nothing. There remained in his mind an inevitable duality between the maker and that which was made. The Demiurge on that account had to have something to work with, and that something was formless matter. In order to organize it he needed a model, and the model was the Idea of the Beautiful (which I capitalize to show that it was not the idea of the Demiurge but a pre-existent, timeless idea independent of all minds). The beautiful was the logical, rational and intelligible, in short, logical order. The God of Genesis is not described as meditating on the model in accordance with which the world would be built. He simply pronounced His word, "Let there be light." He was above all a will, not a reason, a superhuman and omnipotent will, and His fiat sufficed to bring into existence whatever He wished. The purposes of the Demiurge, however, are guided by logic not desire. This would make him subordinate to rationality. In the slogans of the thirteenth century, He made the world because it was good; it was not good simply because He made it. For this reason *Timaeus* is a set of inferences; it is not a history. There is no hexaemeron in Plato. The inferences, as given in *Timaeus* (31B), run about as follows: If something is to come into being, it must be corporeal, for only the corporeal has a beginning in time. The incorporeal, e.g., mathematical figures, are timeless and have neither beginning nor end. But if that which is to come into being is corporeal, then it will be visible and tangible. And if it is visible it must,—according to the physics of that day—be igneous, for only the fiery accounts for light and hence for vision. And if it is tangible, it must have a degree of solidity, and hence would be earthy, for the element earth is the solid. Thus the Demiurge could not have organized a different world because a different world would have been impossible. The one remaining problem of importance was, "What sorts of things would be made?" And the answer, which had more influence than any other one sentence in European thought, was that all possibilities must be

197

realized (*Timaeus*, 29E). This sentence, which the late Professor Lovejoy called the Principle of Plenitude and whose history he wrote in his *The Great Chain of Being*, was an assumption on Plato's part and an assumption that was to be denied by Aristotle.

No such restrictions bound the Mosaic God. Yahweh created the matter of the world by His fiat. The question of its form and order does not come up. Its goodness was seen by the Creator, but no reasons are given for thinking it good. The world becomes a challenge to men because of Adam's fall, and a challenge which must be faced daily. The Fall of Man was inevitable if nothing happens against God's will and if He is also omniscient, and the problem of evil immediately presents itself to the philosopher. Adam was given a command and failed to obey it. And throughout the historical portions of the Old Testament it is man's obedience or disobedience to the divine commandments that determines the course of history. In contrast with this, the Demiurge gives no command to mankind. Man, like God, is committed to reason and neither can go against the principles of rationality without evil happening. In the Bible no reason need be given by God for His commandments, and in the story of Job the cause of his troubles, which is concealed from its victim, is his ability to withstand temptation. Oddly enough, it is God who is tempted by Satan to try Job.

There are here, it is easy to see, two fundamental conflicts in belief. Aside from the matter of Creation, it is clear that, on the one side, we have a belief in the fundamentality of reason and, on the other, that of will. This was not the last time that the conflict between rationalism and voluntarism was to be fought. Both sides overlooked the basic flaw in their premises. The rationalist must start from unproved premises, and the question of why they are chosen cannot be answered rationally. Their selection is extralogical. The voluntarist, like Machiavelli or Nietzsche, maintains that the will creates right and wrong: what I wish is right because I wish it. Hence anything could happen in a world governed by a voluntaristic God, and almost everything did happen in the Bible. But if that were so, then there would be no predictable order in nature. Moreover, some wishes— that is, some human wishes—are inherently unrealizable. If one cannot, for instance, make a circular square, there must be something to logic which is extravolitional. Plato thought he knew that the beautiful was the intelligible, and from there on it was plain sailing. But the beautiful was not in question for Moses. Whatever God chose to make would be good because He had made it. Nevertheless, for centuries Christian theologians spoke of *Timaeus* as if it were a preparation for the reception of the Gospels, a *praeparatio evangelica.* Yet, as we have tried to show, its God, the Demiurge, is far from being the God of either Testament.

Similar remarks can be made of the Unmoved Mover of Aristotle, who provided the model for the God of St. Thomas Aquinas, a model that retained some of the characteristics of the Demiurge. The Unmoved Mover, like the Demiurge, was not a creator. For Aristotle, the universe had always existed and would never come to an end. There was consequently no question of how it began. Moreover, the Unmoved Mover had no feelings; he was the object of love but loved nothing except possibly himself. His activity consisted in thinking about thinking, which to Aristotle was the noblest form of activity. This being so, the government of the world had to be uniform and predictable, for no miracles could occur in a cosmos that was governed by the laws of thought. It was also impossible for him to be incarnated in a man, though a man might strive to approximate his immobility and intellectual perfection. He might be called the purpose and end of the universe, that for which the universe existed, the "form" of the universe in Aristotelian language, but the one form which was separate from its matter.

One cannot understand Aristotle unless one accepts his rational technique. In proving the existence of an Unmoved Mover, he makes a distinction, which he believes is basic, between acting and being acted upon, the agent and the patient. Action for him presupposes an agent, just as passion, or being acting upon, presupposes a patient. The distinction probably comes out of Greek grammar which, like English and a number of other languages, has an active and a passive form of many verbs and both "voices" require subjects. When a distinction is rooted in language it is taken for granted and its rightness seems self-evident. In any event, once this distinction is accepted, there is reason to believe that there are four sorts of substances or subjects in the world: (1) the moved (or passive) and unmoving (incapable of acting); (2) the moved and moving (active); (3) the un-moved (impassive) and moving; and (4) the unmoved and unmoving. We shall see below how a ninth-century philosopher took over these distinctions as a basis for his philosophy.

It was the unmoved and moving which took the place of Plato's Demiurge who in Christian philosophy was identified with God. To speak of a mover who is not moved is to speak of something incorporeal, for the cor-poreal in ancient thought could always be acted upon, whereas the incorporeal never could. If then the world is governed—moved—by an unmoved mover, that denies that in causation there is a reaction from effect to cause. For instance, when one billiard ball hits another, the second moves off, but so does the first in accordance with the third law of motion. The reaction of causation upon a cause is one that Aristotle faced squarely and solved by making the Unmoved Mover a final cause, a purpose or end. If a final cause is accountable for change, then it may remain unchanged while the change it accounts for is going on. The purpose that a man has in walking down a road is not changed by his walking. But the man who is doing the walking is changed by the fatigue or ex-hilaration of the exercise. The cosmos has stability in the sense that its laws are unvariable and do not change with time. Aristotle thought that this uniformity was that for which the world exists, and it became therefore its final cause. The great difficulty was why Aristotle should have thought it was separable from the world.

There is no explicit answer to this question in the works which we have by Aristotle. But the fact that the life of the Unmoved Mover is thinking about thinking no doubt indicates that there runs through all thought, regardless of its subject matter, a set of laws which were the framework of Aristotle's logic. If these laws were really universal and everlasting, then they would be considered to be separate from that which they controlled. Like an algebraic formula or a geometrical theorem, their truth is not embedded in the material world. And hence, even if Aristotle's God were no more than the cosmic order, He would still be alone, apart from matter.

Polytheism by the end of the pagan period was of little interest to philosophers. They all spoke of the gods when customary, but the Epicureans, for instance, believed that divine beings could take no interest in the affairs of men. It was common for philosophers to speak of Zeus or of God unqualified. At the same time, when Stoicism and Epicureanism were becoming religions as well as philosophies, Pythagoreanism rose to a point of influence and God became replaced by *the One*. The One in early Pythagorean thinking was the source of all numbers. The numbers flowed out of the One to form the first decade. The rest of the system of whole numbers was simply the reduplication of the decade. But this process was symbolized by a figure in the form of a triangle, the *tetraktys.*

This symbol is probably the source of a later idea, a metaphor, that all things flowed out of an original source, were not created but emanated. The fantastic fiddling with number symbolism, with perfect numbers, virgin numbers, male and female numbers need not concern us here. What does concern us is the name, *the One,* which in the works of Plotinus, a Neoplatonist of the third century, became synonymous with what the Christians were calling God. The One, moreover, was not only the source of all being, but superior to all in goodness and beauty. He was the most real of beings, the *ens realissimum* in medieval Latin. Plato had spoken of "the really real," but no one before Philo Judaeus had thought that there were degrees of reality. It now could be asked not whether a thing was real or illusory but how much reality it had. This is like saying that the closer a hand-drawn circle comes to having radii of equal length, the more circular it is. Most people would say this was nonsense and that a circle had to be circular or it was not a circle. If one admits that there are degrees of reality, there must be a standard of perfection, of the really real. The One became that standard. A thing, then, was real or unreal to the extent that it approached the reality of the One. But in what sense of the word was the One real? In the sense that it was the source of everything else, was timeless, incorporeal, and a universal predicate. Everything that exists is a unit.

There are obviously several kinds of unity: unity of origin, as in a family and its descendants; unity of matter, as in a group of marble statues; unity of purpose, as in an athletic team; unity of pattern or structure, as in certain Greek temples or American skyscrapers or, for that matter, vertebrate animals; organic unity, where all the parts of an animal work together, each serving the whole; the unity of destiny, as in a group of convicts in Death Row or the Senior Class just before Commencement. But the word "unity" has a kind of emotional aura about it, so that if something is unified it is said to be better than it would be if disunified. Thus a novel or any other work of art is supposed to be unified if it is to be praiseworthy, and even people have been told to unify their lives, to give them one purpose, to hitch their wagon to a star, or to seek their identity, as if they must have one and not several. Hence, to find at the top of the pyramid the One was to find there also the source of values.

The values, as we have suggested earlier in this sketch, according to the Bible were in the decrees of God. How to find them was clear enough for all to read in the Decalogue and the Sermon on the Mount. If details were needed to specify particular situations, one had only to turn to Leviticus and Deuteronomy and, as far as the Jews were concerned, the Talmud. But neither Greece nor Rome had a god who laid down moral laws, and hence the philosophers of these countries had to reason to the nature of their deities. Oddly enough, though they differed on many points, they all—Epicureans, Stoics, Skeptics, Platonists, Aristotelians—agreed that the end of life was self-sufficiency, autarky. A man must live so that he will be independent of all things external to himself, even family, friends, and society as a whole. This program, if followed, would lead to a withdrawal from all responsibilities and hence could be strictly followed by no one. The man of wealth and the pauper might approximate it and Diogenes the Cynic almost reached it. Because of this ideal the pagan philosophies were an inducement to disintegration in spite of their including, with the exception of the Skeptics and the Epicureans, a single divine being. The Stoics had emphasized man's citizenship in the Cosmopolis, the City of Zeus, and the brotherhood of man. But the duties of such citizenship were not altruistic; they were self-centered. In short, there was no sacred text to serve as guide.

In that respect the Christians had the advantage. Though they quarreled over the interpretation of that text, and quarreled mightily, nevertheless each sect had a definite creed and the outcome of the doctrinal battles, which did little credit to the followers of the Prince of Peace, was one universal (catholic) creed for all men. The opening of this creed is, as all Christians know, "I believe in one God." This God was the creator of "all things visible and invisible." He was a judge of men's conduct and would punish and reward it as it deserves. But He was also a person, very like but infinitely superior to human beings. He could be, indeed should be, loved. He could be prayed to as if He were another man willing to listen. One could communicate with Him, not necessarily asking Him for favors, but simply opening one's heart to Him as to a friend. He was incarnate in Jesus Christ and born of a virgin. He was crucified and rose from the dead. And if one was a Trinitarian, as most Christians have been, He was identical with His Son and with the Holy Spirit, though different in person.

All this is put down here to depict as freely as possible what a religious God is and to show how different He is from a metaphysical God, a first cause, an Unmoved Mover, a Platonic Demiurge, the One. The metaphysical God is not a person, is not anthropomorphic, not a creator, could not be incarnated, is not one of three persons. He is required to form a system of thought, when he is required at all. But he is only required by those men who find faith insufficient. Few pagans, one imagines, worried about the existence of the gods; they took them over from tradition, sacrificed to them, consulted oracles, looked for omens, took the myths in their stride as Christians take the miracles and mysteries. But for reasons of which we are ignorant, there are always some men who prefer reason to faith. Rather than believe first and understand later, they wish to understand and then believe if possible. The compulsion to make sense out of what one believes is the impetus to all philosophy and science. We accept certain things as common sense, such things as the existence of an external world, or of other people's minds, or of the past and the future. But we want reasons for accepting common sense. The problems of metaphysics, as given in an ordinary textbook, seem absurd to the philosophic layman. And for getting along in our daily jobs they are absurd. If someone asks me why I believe in the real existence of what took place yesterday and I reply that I am relying on my memory, I am immediately enmeshed in a complicated argument about the tests for the validity of memories. Sometimes my memory does indeed play me false. But how do I know that it has played me false? As soon as I try to answer that insidious question, I am involved in theories of truth and the problem of error. Man is a question-raising animal, though men differ in the degree of curiosity they will manifest. But there are in every age some men who do not cease to question; they want to know the grounds for their beliefs even when the beliefs are admittedly based on faith.

It was this tendency that merged the metaphysical God with the religious God. One of the earliest attempts at doing this was that of Erigena, of which we have already spoken. Dividing the world in four sets of things, the created and the uncreating, the created and creating, the uncreated and creating, and the uncreated and uncreating, he found himself turning his one God into all four. For first He was uncreated but creating, the primal cause of everything else for whom there was no anteced- ent cause. Second, He was uncreated and uncreating as the final cause, that for which all else existed, like the Unmoved Mover. But in the class of beings that are created and creating, animate objects, there must be some explanation of why they act as they do, for creation is a divine attribute. Hence Erigena speaks of God creating in the created, as if His presence would alone explain the generative power and activity observable to all. In the class of things which are created but do not create, inanimate nature, as long as they exist and have any reality, that reality must reflect the creative power of God. And since for Erigena creation *ex nihilo* is what creation means, this class of beings must emanate from God's being and hence participate in it. Not only do the heavens declare the glory of God but they are themselves part of His glory.

It was clear after a century or so that Erigena was close to being a pantheist. For the distinction between God and His creatures was almost nonexistent. More- over, creation was an eternal process, not an act that occurred at a certain date. For God, being immutable, could not have changed from being a noncreator to being a creator. The subtleties of his dialectic could not save Erigena from condemnation and his book was ordered to be burned in 1225. As Father Copleston says in his *History of Philosophy* (Vol. 2, p. 133), he "makes no clear cut distinction between theology and philosophy."

In this he was close to Spinoza. There happen to be certain principles, those stated for instance in the Creed, that must be taken as either premises or conclusions. Monotheism is one of these. But then philosophy can enter and can reason to the nature of the one God. Yet philosophy has to have some tests of evidence, just as science does. And experience shows us that when it is applied to religion, it fails to preserve the Christian's Creed. It comes face to face with sentences that it cannot demonstrate and that it has to accept as mysteries, the dogma of the Blessed Trinity being one of them.

Though Erigena can be safely called the initiator of the merger of the two Gods, the most extraordinary philosophical interpretation of Christianity is obviously that of St. Thomas Aquinas. He sets out among other things to prove the existence of God, and in his five proofs, assuming they are valid, we find that God is the first cause of motion; that He is the first efficient cause or the primordial agent of all acts, not merely of motion; that He is a being who is self-determined and the source of all necessary beings; that He is the standard of perfection in all things that admit of degrees; and, finally, that He is the directing power of all things that act purposively—and even the things without knowledge, material things, act for an end. Assuming, as we have said, that these proofs are valid, we find ourselves confronted with five Gods, for it is not evident that the primordial cause of all motion is identical with the final cause of all purposes. Nor is it evident that any of the other conclusions are logically entailed in one another. What is even more curious is that there is nothing in the Creed which implies that God is any of these things. St. Thomas had proved the existence of a first mover, a first efficient cause, a standard for all values, a source of necessity as opposed to contingency, and a single coordinating power of all final causes. Even if he had proved that all these were coalesced into one superhuman person, he would not have proved the existence of the God of the Creed.

After the rise of Protestantism the number of metaphysical Gods increased. There was Rousseau's God who was discovered by his heart; Voltaire's, who organized and governed the universe like a constitutional monarch; Kant's, who was a necessary postulate of the practical reason; Hegel's, who was the absolute idea realized eternally in the dialectical process; Royce's who was the Beloved Community; Whitehead's, who was the principle of concretion; Tillich's, who was the ground of being— and these are only a handful of those which come to mind. These are all metaphysical Gods, not religious Gods. No man could pray to any of them. None of them could have delivered the Decalogue. None could perform miracles or be incarnated. In short, God had become a name for whatever principle of unity a philosopher could discover in the universe. The outcome of all this was the announcement that God was dead, as indeed He was if He was one of the gods constructed by metaphysical dialectic. For none of them is the God of Moses, to say nothing of the God of the four evangelists.

It was argued by Pseudo-Dionysius (A.D. fifth century) that God's nature could be reached only by telling what He was not, the so-called negative way. The reason for this was an assumption that God was not the biblical God at all but, rather, the omnipresent spirit which included all things in His nature. The whole of things cannot be defined, for any terms of description would have to come from within the whole. But the biblical God, of both Jews and Christians, transcends the world and is not the whole. There are to be sure verses in Scripture that could be interpreted metaphysically, such as, "I am what I am," or, "In Him we live and move and have our being." But we have already seen what the former phrase probably meant, and as for the latter, it is human beings of whom St. Paul is speaking, not all the world. We can take literally the Pauline phrase, as given in the Vulgate, *omnia in omnibus* ("all in all things"), and interpret it to mean that God is the God of Deism, if we wish, but our desire will not turn St. Paul into an eighteenth-century thinker. The philosophic transformation of the one God of the Old Testament into a multiplicity of metaphysical gods has had the effect of denying the reality of that which the procedure was supposed to prove.

·10·

The Microcosm

The idea that man is a microcosm, a little world, as contrasted with the big world, the macrocosm, is of interest to the history of ideas mainly as an example of the extension of a basic metaphor. In this case some human trait or group of human traits is projected into the nonhuman world and used as an explanatory device. Once the projection is accomplished, it takes on an objective air and is thought of as an integral part of the world or, in one example, of the state. For this to be successful, some analogy must be found to exist between human nature and the external world, and the best example of that is obviously what Ruskin called the pathetic fallacy.

It is a peculiarity of Hebrew poetry, as we have it preserved in the Old Testament, that the writers seldom commit this fallacy. They are not unobservant of the

212

natural scene, far from it, but they do not usually endow it with a life of its own. There are a few verses which might seem to be an exception to this generalization. Psalm 110:3 speaks of the womb of the morning; Psalm 114:3-4, says that "the sea saw it [the escape of Israel from Egypt] and fled: Jordan was driven back. The mountains skipped like rams, the little hills like lambs." In Job the morning stars sing together, and in the Song of Songs 4:16, the Bride sings: "Awake, O north wind; and come, thou south; blow upon my garden, that the spices thereof may flow out." But almost always the landscape is thought of as God's creation and whatever life it has was given to it by God. The heavens declare His glory, not their own, and throughout the Psalms, or the book of Job or even the Song of Songs, we are bidden to see the hand of the Creator in creation.

Greek poetry was entirely different on this score. Not only were the heavens alive with inherent vitality, but the clouds, the winds, the seas and rivers and springs, the trees and mountains, indeed every feature of the environment was invested with divinity and with a divinity that was individuated. This went so far that the names of certain gods could be substituted for their domains: thus grain could be called Ceres and wine Bacchus, as if their gifts were identical with themselves. One can see this train of thought best exemplified in Ovid's *Metamorphoses*, where the characters of trees, flowers, rivers, and beasts are interpreted as the invasion of these beings by semidivine or human creatures. One might say with excusable exaggeration that for the pagan the whole of nature was alive, not that the spirit of the one universal God was present in it, as a pantheist might say, but as a community of souls, some of which were so individuated that they might be in conflict with others.

The projection of human traits into the natural world was avoided by the Hebrews by making their God the supernatural model, so superior in wisdom, power, and goodness that men were but faint replicas of Him, created though they were in His image and likeness. If a drought occurred, it was not because an angry river-god had withheld his fructifying waters, but because God was punishing men for their sins. The pagan might sacrifice to make amends, and so indeed might the ancient Hebrew, but the deity to whom they were sacrificing, though anthropomorphic in both cases, was in all other respects different. In Job, God visits Job with horrors, but they are not a punishment for some defect in ceremony, some failure to observe the proper omens. They served as a moral test. A pagan in similar circumstances would probably have felt that he had omitted some gestures of respect to some more or less unidentified god. But as pagan culture developed and the philosophers gained some influence, Zeus began to assume a larger place in ancient theology and became the supreme father of gods and men, governing the world according to law. Pagan writings illustrate more and more clearly the belief that man's fate was determined by divine powers. These powers might at times be revealed in oracles and omens and dreams, but they might also be exercised without their victims knowing it. It was in vain that Plato, Aristotle, the Epicureans, and the Stoics preached an ethics in which the good could be attained by purely human means; the average pagan still moved in a world controlled by forces which were either friendly or hostile, and that in a capricious manner. The God of Old Testament also moved in mysterious ways, but so long as a man obeyed the commandments, lived righteously, all would go well. And the way to live righteously was written down for all to read, not only in the Decalogue but also in Leviticus and Deuteronomy. When one reads, for instance, Xenophon, whether in the *Anabasis* or the *Hellenica*, one is amazed to see how much care he and his associates took to observe the omens before taking a decision. Had he been a Hebrew instead of a Greek, there would have been no need for him to consult the gods, Zeus or Artemis or Apollo. For the righteous man might make a mistake, but his righteousness would be a guarantee against disaster. The difficulty was that no man was perfect.

If this approximates the truth closely enough to be acceptable, it is easy to see why Hebrew poetry is so devoid of the pathetic fallacy. For brooks to chatter and mountains to frown, the human element must be in them. What is of interest to us here is that the ideas of the philosophers were not always so influential as those of the common people. It was the latter who accepted the myths and who saw in nature a collection of anthro-

pomorphic spirits, often as wicked as wicked men, sometimes beneficent, but all interested in blackmail or
rewards. Yet the philosophers too shared this point of
view, even if in a more depersonalized form. For they
saw human energy in the form of causation and human
purpose in teleology. To speak of a cause producing its
effect is to talk in anthropomorphic terms, however refined, just as it is to say, for instance, that trees have
leaves in order to effect photosynthesis. Man's power to
make things, to change the course of nature, and to
repair the damage made by disasters such as floods and
earthquakes is undeniable. It is also undeniable that men
can act in order to achieve certain ends. But when the
nonhuman world is endowed with these same faculties,
one has begun to talk in metaphorical language. Thus
in the earliest forms of scientific explanation in the Occidental tradition, human nature was projected into the
nonhuman world. Nature in its changes behaved as if
it were a human being.

All science must begin with analogies. The similarities that exist among things and events give the scientist
a clue to possible identities which he will then use as a
basis for classification. Strictly speaking, no two things are
exactly alike and it is all a question of what the scientist
is going to do with the information that he has assembled.
For purposes of prediction, the way things behave is
more important than the way they look. It is unlikely
that scientists would make collections of green things or
round things and think that they could formulate inter-

esting generalizations about them. But if they noticed that certain things turned green after exposure to sunlight or certain animals rolled themselves into balls in the presence of human beings, they might have the beginning of something worth studying. If the similarities are those between human beings and nonhuman things, then it will be normal to explain the behavior of the latter as if it were an example of the former. This may be why there is no science in the Old Testament. Science emerged, and perhaps could only emerge, out of Greek mythology. And the warfare between science and religion has continued to this day.

Among the early projections of human nature into the world of science was the "Love" and "Strife" of Empedocles (5th century B.C.), which we would translate into modern language as "attraction" and "repulsion." The poetic connotation of Love and Strife is obviously vastly different from that of attraction and repulsion, but the denotation is the same. It sounds more sophisticated to say that the magnet attracts the piece of steel than to say that the piece of steel loves the magnet. Yet when Aristotle, surely one of the most sophisticated of ancient thinkers, tried to explain the order that exists in the cosmos, an order dependent on the Unmoved Mover, the best he could do was to say that the universe is attracted by the Unmoved Mover as the Lover is attracted by the Beloved. In the *Divine Comedy*, this becomes the last line of the *Paradiso*: "The love that moves the sun and the other stars."

In the Hebraic tradition the most radical projection of human nature was clearly the idea of the one God who was the creator of the universe and its lawgiver. Though we have always been warned of talking about God in human terms, yet He is a personal God in whose image and likeness we have been made. The Greeks had no creation story: the philosophers thought that the world was everlasting and the mythographers spoke of it as self-made, in one account a cosmic egg floating on chaos. But both agreed in thinking that behind the phenomena of perception was a spirit, or spirits, similar though superior to human beings. These could be thought of as having reason, will, and perception, and some of them had foreknowledge of everything that was to happen. When a philosopher like Xenophanes (late sixth century B.C.) ridiculed such beliefs, his effect on popular thought was nil. And though the Unmoved Mover of Aristotle is about as depersonalized as any god has ever been, nevertheless he was spoken of in personal terms as "he." But, for that matter, Newton himself, who refused to discuss the nature of the force of gravitation, believed that if there was one law describing the motion of all things, it must be the decree of a supernatural lawgiver.

Man had a body as well as a mind or spirit. Apparently Plato first pointed out the kinship between the human body and the universe. In *Philebus* (29) Socrates points out that just as there are four elements in the universe, so there are in us. In us they are weak and mixed and unworthy of the power which the nature of the body ought to give them. But the corresponding elements in the cosmos are pure and strong, and it is they which nourish the elements that are in us. Since this much of a correspondence has been established, one must pass on to a further one. Just as the material elements in our bodies are held together and cooperate because they are subject to the soul, so the four elements in the universe as a whole must be organized by a corresponding soul, the Soul of the World. Thus, Plato's Zeus and the other divinities are organizing spirits, wisdom and reason. This was apparently the literary source of the idea that we are discussing.

There was, it is easy to see, a possibility that two sets of parallelisms would be imagined to exist between man and the cosmos, one physical and the other psychical. The possibility was soon actualized. In *Philebus* (30A) Plato maintains that just as the body resembles the body of the universe, so the soul of the universe must have wisdom (*sophia*) and intelligence (*nous*). One could pass either from the human being to the cosmos or from the cosmos to the human being. So in *Timaeus* (30) the world is said to be an image of the Demiurge, endowed with soul and intelligence, and thus it duplicates the individual human being.

The actual word "microcosm" (little world) was first used by Plato's pupil, Aristotle, in his *Physics* (252*b*, 26). He is arguing in this passage about the cause of motion in the cosmos. His sentence reads, "If [self-initiated] motion can occur in an animal, the little world, why not in the larger one?" There are at least three things to be noticed about this sentence: (1) the animal is for the first time called a microcosm; (2) an animal trait is projected into the cosmos, which later, in Stoicism, was to be called a great animal (*mega zoon*); (3) the microcosm is not specifically man. Oddly enough, the third of these was not developed. When one comes upon the word "microcosm," one can be sure that it means "man."

A similar parallelism without the word is said to have been found in Democritus, a contemporary of Socrates, though the opinion is probably wrong. He too was said to have referred to man as a little world, on the ground that just as the cosmos consists of three kinds of being— the divine who rule, the human who rule and are ruled, and the beasts which are only ruled—so man consists of reason, emotion, and desire, which correspond to the three kinds of being in the cosmos. But in Aristotle too, in his psychology, we find that man's psyche sums up the three kinds of souls, the vegetative, the sensitive (animal), and the rational (human). Here instead of reading human traits into nature, Aristotle crowds the three "kingdoms" into man.

It was Plato also who began the tradition of conceiving of the state as a large man. In his dialogue the *Republic*, he begins by asking what justice is and points out that it will be easier to find the answer if one takes the just state as a model rather than the just individual, since the latter would be too small in scale. Then, since

all men are composed of three faculties (appetite, iras-
cibility (usually translated "spiritedness"), and reason,
there must be classes of people in the state who correspond to these faculties. For just as an individual must
eat and reproduce his kind, must defend himself against
hostile forces, and must reason, so the state has artisans
who are predominantly appetitive, soldiers who are iras-
cible, and philosophers who are rational. Unfortunately,
as Socrates points out, these types of men are not kept
at their proper work, but as things go, the artisans do
the reasoning, such as it is, or the soldiers win control,
and one has either a nation of pigs or a nation constantly
on the warpath. What is wanted is a state in which the
rational men run the state and direct things so that each
class does its appropriate work and does not usurp the
position of others. This conceptual model of the state as
an enlarged human being was carried over into the Middle Ages, with extravagant detail.

The correspondence between the individual man and
the cosmos must have become a commonplace by the
end of the pagan era, for we find it in both Philo Judaeus
(1st century) and the *Hermetica.* Discussing the biblical
verse that man is made in the image and likeness of
God, Philo says (*De opificio mundi* xxiii, 69) that the
resemblance does not lie in our bodies, far from it, but
in our possession of intelligence (*nous*), which rules us
exactly as God rules the world as a whole. In this way
Philo avoids the correspondence between animals and
the cosmos, for animals do not possesss intelligence.

221

Moreover, he flatly says (*Legum allegoria* i, xxix, 91-2) that we may think of God as the soul of the whole, thus identifying Him with the Neoplatonic *anima mundi*. And in *The Migration of Abraham* (*De migratione* xxxiii, 185) he makes the correspondence more detailed by arguing that by reflecting upon one's household, a symbol for the body, one can see that there is a duality in it between the master and those that are subject to him, the living and the lifeless, the rational and the irrational, the immortal and the mortal, the better and the worse. This will show us that in the cosmos as a whole there is a God corresponding to the mind; God who is the master, the life, the immortal, the best, the rational; and so on. And just as the mind rules the body, so God rules the world. Moreover, he uses terms similar to those of Aristotle when he says that man is a small world and the world a large man (*Quid rerum?* xxix-xxxi, 146-56).[1]

But there was a profound difference between the position of God in the Platonists and Neoplatonists, on the one hand, and in the Jewish and Christian philosophers, on the other. The former could think of God as the Soul of the World, for they were not committed to any thesis

[1] For other passages in Philo, showing how common the metaphor had become, see *De opificio mundi* xxvii, 82, "Man is a little heaven"; also *De plantatione* vii, 28, in which our organs are compared to trees, the organs of the world; *De Abrahamo* xvi, 74 and xlvi, 272, where the wise man is compared to the pilot of a ship, the ruler of a city, the general in war, the soul in the body, the mind in the soul, heaven in the world, and God in heaven.

of creation. Plato's Demiurge did not create the world; he gave organization and form to already existing matter. But according to the Bible, God existed before there was any world, though the word "before" arouses metaphysical questions when applied to a timeless being. Consequently, for Philo in particular the correspondence was a figure of speech and really a likeness between men and God, not between a man and the cosmos. The situation was thus very different from that of the pagans. We have already mentioned Aristotle's theory that the human soul epitomized the three kinds of soul that existed in the world. But more than that each lower order was the potentiality of the order next above it, so that nutrition and generation, which were common to all life, existed for the sake of sensation, common only to animals and men, and sensation existed for the sake of reason, which was man's differentia. It was this pattern probably, we cannot say certainly, that was more influential than any other in suggesting a close correspondence between man and the world as a whole. It should be mentioned that there is a fragment of Philolaos, a Pythagorean who lived at least a generation before Aristotle, which makes a closer parallel than Aristotle's. Philolaos is supposed to have said that the brain, the heart, the navel, and the genitals corresponded to mankind, beasts, vegetation, and the whole of creation, being respectively the seat of intelligence, psychical and perceptual activity, growth and the formation of the fetus, and genesis.[2] But

[2] This fragment comes from the *Theologoumena Arithmeticae* of Iamblichus (4th century), ed. De Falco (Leipzig, 1922), p. 25.

the fragment is too obscure in its intention to stand close interpretation and is, moreover, of doubtful authenticity. It is, however, evidence of the interest certain writers had in making a correspondence between man and the world. So in the more rhapsodical language of the *Hermetica* are passages which say that man is that of which Nature is the image (*Poimandres* i, 12, 31), that as eternity is the image of God, so the cosmos is the image of eternity, the sun of the cosmos, and man of the sun (*Nous to Hermes, Poimandres* xi, 15) and that from his divine composition man is called a cosmos (*Asclepius* x).[3]

By the time of Seneca (1st century A.D.) the game had been elaborated to the point that the earth itself was talked of in terms of the human body. In his *Natural Questions* (iii, xv, 1) we find Seneca saying that just as we have veins and arteries, so has the earth. Our veins carry blood and our arteries carry air, and similarly in the earth there are conduits carrying water and air. And just as we have other "humors," brain, marrow, mucus, saliva, tears, so has the earth, of which some harden and become minerals, gold and silver, bitumen and "such like things." If you open a vein, blood spurts out; if you do the same to the earth, a spring or river will arise. Moreover, says Seneca (*Ibid.*, xvi), just as the human

[3] The Hermetic writings date from the end of the pagan period to the end of the second century A.D., though some of the writings may be much earlier and some later. The references in my text are to the edition of Festugière and Nock, Paris, Vols. i and ii, 1960, Vols. iii and iv, 1954.

body manifests certain periodicities, quartan fever, gout, menstruation, the time of gestation, so does the earth, as springs overflow and dry up. In fact, one might find a parallel to the humanizing of the world in those representations of the seasons, in which spring is always young, summer more mature, and winter a trembling old man. But Seneca himself does not carry the analogy to that point. The earth could grow old and indeed had already done so according to common belief, a belief that lasted well into modern times, but that it went through infancy and youth is not found in the remaining literature of the ancients.[4]

Meanwhile, the pseudo-science of astrology was spreading and, as rational philosophy and science declined, superstition took their place. It is one thing to maintain that man's fate is determined by forces over which he has no control; it is another to project into the heavenly bodies the features of human psychology. This was done in two ways: first, by assigning to the planets certain human traits; second, by assigning to the signs of the zodiac portions of the human body over which they would have that mysterious control that is discoverable from a horoscope. The psychological traits of the planets survive in our ordinary vocabulary: saturnine, jovial, mercurial, lunatic, venereal. Since Neptune was not discovered until 1846, we do not call people neptunian,

[4] For the senescence of the earth in antiquity, see A. O. Lovejoy and G. Boas, *Primitivism . . . in Antiquity* (Baltimore, 1935), Index, under "Senescence."

and the planet has been a problem to astrologers ever since.[5] This implied that the planetary system, which in the early days included the sun and moon as planets, was like a human psyche with all the types of emotion that a human being might have. It is worth pointing out that no planet stood for or controlled the reason or perception. Perhaps that is reserved for Pluto. But in one of the Hermetic fragments preserved by Stobaeus (5th century A.D.) there is a curious parallel between the seven planets and human traits which says that the planets are in us. That is why we breathe etherized breath, shed tears, laugh, grow angry, beget children, speak, sleep, and have desires. For tears come from the Kronos within us, generation from Zeus, speech from Hermes, anger from Ares, sleep from Luna, desire from Aphrodite, and laughter from the Sun.[6]

When it came to the constellations of the zodiac, the parallelism is even stranger, and it is worth conjecturing that the idea derived from the passage of Philolaos or Pseudo-Philolaos and some author upon whom he was dependent. In traditional astrology the Ram controls the head, the Bull the neck, the Twins the arms, the Lion the shoulders, the Crab the breast, the Maiden the entrails, the Scales the buttocks, the Scorpion the genitals, the Centaur the thighs, the Goat the knees, Aquarius the legs, and the Fish the feet. This was somewhat

[5] See Louis MacNeice, *Astrology* (Garden City, N. Y., 1964), p. 66.
[6] Stobaeus, I, 5. 14; ed. Hense-Wachsmuth (Berlin, 1958), Vol. I, p. 77.

like the arrangement of the universe and the Sephirot in the Cabala, of which we reproduce a chart (see p. 228). However absurd these correlations may be, men cast horoscopes, saw psychic traits in the spatial relations of planets and constellations, and in spite of warnings from the Church, saw their destiny written in the stars. A superstition as powerful as this cannot be swept aside in a history of ideas. The projection of the human body in the heavens, the endowment of the planets with emotion, all made the solar system, which before Copernicus was the only universe man knew, a great man in contrast to us little men.

Though Xenophanes said that if oxen and horses had hands and could paint, they would represent their gods as larger oxen and horses, he did not anticipate how detailed a description of the cosmic soul would be made some centuries later. By the third century A.D., in the work of Plotinus, we have the universe itself, an emanation of something akin to the human soul, the One, out of whom flowed two beings who were the source of everything else. These beings were called the Intelligence (*nous*) and the Soul of the World (*anima mundi*). From the former came those eternal patterns of all possibilities, known as the Ideas, and from the latter all the souls of men. The souls of men in turn, according to the lives they led on earth, might re-emerge in the bodies of beasts. The production of the world was, as we have said, emanation. The material world was a degeneration of this spiritual or psychical world "up there." The meta-

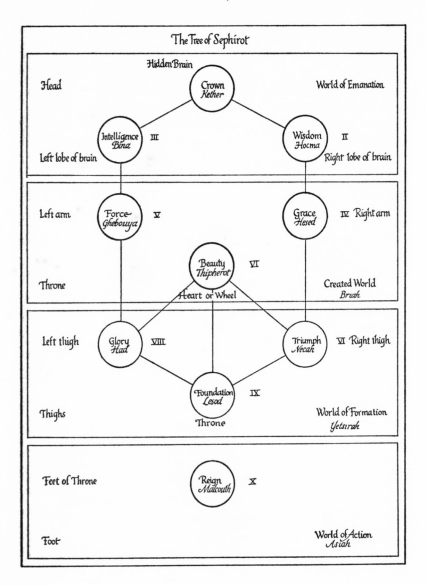

The Tree of Sephirot

Hidden Brain

Head — World of Emanation

Crown
Kether

Intelligence
Bina — III

Wisdom
Hocma — II

Left lobe of brain — Right lobe of brain

Left arm — Force
Ghebouya — V

Grace
Hesed — IV Right arm

Beauty
Thipherot — VI

Throne — Created World
Briah

Heart or Wheel

Left thigh — Glory
Had — VIII

Triumph
Necah — VI Right thigh

Foundation
Lesod — IX

Thighs — World of Formation
Yetsirah

Throne

Feet of Throne — Reign
Malcouth — X

Foot — World of Action
Asiah

228

phor used by Plotinus was the light emanating from a candle and passing off into darkness. But the whole scheme itself was a larger metaphor. Whereas certain ancient philosophers, Democritus and his school, built up the contents of the mind from sensations acquired from contact with the material world, Plotinus and his school reversed the process: one's mind at birth was stocked with ideas which later were recognized in their imperfect exemplifications on earth. This was not so arbitrary a move as it might seem. It appears reasonable to say that if we did not have sense organs, we would know nothing. But on the other hand, the sense organs alone would not tell us what we know. At a minimum, knowledge demands classification, and when we rise from immediate contact with colors and sounds and such to more general knowledge, there is a genuine problem of where the principles of classification come from. Plato himself, in his dialogue *Meno*, raised this problem, and the Neoplatonic tradition developed it to the point of declaring that all general ideas came from within the mind; and in some philosophers, subjective idealists, even the objects of knowledge, sensible matter, were only partly "objective." By the middle of the nineteenth century, in for instance the work of Hans Vaihinger, there was the suggestion that all scientific patterns, patterns by means of which we organize our data, are projections of human characters, just as the ancient concepts of purpose and cause had been.

But no one in this tradition thought of the universe

as an enlarged man. That was left to the fancy of men less given to logic. We cannot in a book of this sort enter into all the details of medieval intellectual history, and so we shall content ourselves with mentioning a few outstanding characteristics.

First, the Cabala. We have already mentioned how the "Sephirotic Tree" is based upon the structure of the human body. But as early as the Aboth (8th or 9th century A.D.), we find R. Natan (Chap. 31) comparing every part of the human body to some feature of the earth: the hair to the forests, the bones to the wood, the lungs to the winds. In the Bahya, the nine spheres correspond to the nine substances, bones and the like, of the human body; the twelve signs of the zodiac represent the twelve apertures, and just as each sign is supervised by a power emanating from and returning to the universal soul, so is every limb of the body governed by some power of the human soul, there being obviously a complete parallelism between the bodies and souls of the individual and the cosmos. A similar point of view, though less fantastic, was expressed by the tenth-century Jewish philosopher, Isaac Israeli.[7] He approached the matter from the axiom that man's duty is to know himself. This approach he apparently borrowed from Al-Kindi who said, "Philosophy is man's knowing himself.
. . . Things are corporeal or non-corporeal; the non-corpo-

[7] I use the translation and commentary of A. Altmann and S. M. Stern, *Isaac Israeli, a Neoplatonic Philosopher of the Early Tenth Century* (Oxford, 1958) (*Scripta Judaica* I).

real things are either substances or accidents; man consists of body, soul, and accidents; soul is a substance, not a body; therefore if man knows himself, he knows body with its accidents, the first accident, and the substance which is not a body; as he knows all these, he knows everything. For this reason the philosophers called man a microcosm." The source of the idea that self-knowledge was cosmic knowledge, is probably a treatise of Porphyry's, *On Know Thyself*, a third-century work. The passage in question runs, "[Those] who say that man is properly called a microcosm say that the term orders knowledge of man. And since man is a microcosm, he is ordered to do nothing other than to philosophize. If then we seriously wish to philosophize without taking a false step, we shall be eager to know ourselves, and we shall acquire a true philosophy from our insight, ascending to the contemplation of the Whole."[8]

Here, then, we have a new approach to the microcosm. It is no longer a comparison, more or less absurd, between man's body and the universal body, but a metaphysical belief that the self and God are related as image to model and that when one knows the image, one also knows the model. Porphyry, as a pupil of Plotinus, believed that the cosmos was a body of which the Soul was the "reality." It is difficult, if not impossible, to clarify just what was meant by reality. But since a man is defined by means of his soul, not his body, so ought the cosmos

[8] Translated from the text as given in Stobaeus, ed. Wachsmuth-Hense (Berlin, 1958), Vol. III, Chap. xxi, No. 27, p. 580.

to be. Thus one would find the famous definition of
man as a featherless biped a bit ludicrous—at least the
ancients did. But to define him as an immortal rational
animal seemed the height of good sense and was repeated
indefinitely by author after author. Since it was believed
that the cosmos had a soul (either God, according to
Philo, or the *anima mundi,* according to the Neoplatonists), it was only proper to make the parallel between
man and the cosmos in their souls.

From that point of view a twelfth-century figure,
Godefroy of Saint Victor (d. 1196), approached the
matter.[9] He makes it clear in his *Microcosmus* (Chap.
18) that man is called a world not because of his body
but because of his spirit. He bases what he has to say on
the parallelism established by St. Augustine in the fifth
century between the ages of the world and those of man,
and he establishes another parallel between these and the
six days of creation. In both authors there is an emphasis
on degeneration. Man was made by God, says Godefroy
(Chap. 12), to have an enduring body,

> that is one able to stand, able not to fall, able not to die.
> Hence he was made superior to all the transitory things
> of this naturally passing world. For all things pass away,
> that is all things of this sublunary world, and do not last.
> For all that comes goes, nor can that remain which
> flows with time. Man however was so created that he
> would not have flowed with flowing things if he had

[9] I use the edition of Philippe Delhaye (Lille and Gembloux,
1951).

232

wished to remain firm. But he did not so wish and began to flow with the flowing, to perish with the perishable, and has been made by himself similar to this perishing world, perishing he too. Nor does he derive the name of this world from his worth but rather from his vileness.

The changes to which man has linked himself are obviously deplorable, for they involve death at the end rather than deathlessness. Hence he is called a microcosm only insofar as his spirit is concerned, for that alone is deathless. Godefroy cannot resist the temptation of pushing the parallelism between man's mind and the days of creation to as extreme a limit as any of the men who saw the microcosm in man's body. For instance, on the first day of creation light appeared, and light corresponds to sensation; on the second day, the waters were divided, and this means that sensation was divided from imagination. But we have a body as well as a mind; this is because of the four elements: two are active and two are passive. The former correspond to our minds, the latter to our bodies. "What comes from without pertains to sensuality; what comes from within pertains to the imagination" (Chap. 24). But then it turns out that the imagination itself has four sources: the *ingenium*, which seeks and finds images of absent things; the *concupiscibilitas*, which attracts the things that are found; the *memoria*, which retains them; and *irascibilitas*, which repels them. But such a multiplicity requires a stabilizer and that is provided in the reason. The reason is analogous to the Spirit of God which stabilizes the world of flux and multiplicity.

We shall omit the other parallels, delightful though they are, to save space, but we should point out that so far man has been described physically, that is, as he exists in nature or in the physical world. There is a much more important side of man to be discussed, that is, man according to grace. God made the world neither for Himself nor for the angels, but for man. There are three forms of grace. The first begins in faith, is perfected through knowledge, and arrives at truth; the second begins in good will, grows through good feelings (*affectiones*), and arrives at virtue; the third begins in potentiality, is perfected through good deeds, and ends in the faculty of good works (Chap. 82). These three are called knowledge of the good, will to achieve the good, and power to do the good.[10] In the world of nature, power comes first, knowledge second, will third, whereas in the world of grace, knowledge is first, will is second, and power comes last (p. 95). Power (*potentia*) comes from the Father, knowledge (*sapientia*) from the Son, and good will (*bonitas*) from the Holy Spirit.

The result of Godefroy's *Microcosmus* is a detailed identification of all the apparent differences that exist in the learning he had acquired. Just as power and wisdom and goodness were identified with the three persons of the Trinity, so were they all coalesced into one as the persons of the Trinity were. The monks of Saint Victor

[10] In Latin, *scire bonum, velle bonum, posse bonum.*

were given to seeing everything under the famous four aspects of the literal, the allegorical, the tropological, and the anagogical, so that for all the mutiplicity of things, they were "in reality" one. This notion of an inner reality was never clearly defined and the analogies which philosophers found among apparently different things were used to demonstrate the inner unity. Thus, to take but one instance, even St. Thomas Aquinas when he discusses the goodness or the lovingkindness of God has to make it clear that these qualities are not identical with such as are manifested in men but can only be known analogically. We should be inclined to take such analogies less seriously today. We are willing, for instance, to talk about the ship of state and perhaps even to speak of the president as its helmsman. But we do not go on, it is to be hoped, to argue statesmanship in terms of navigation, except possibly in cartoons.

The medieval scholar differed profoundly from us in this respect and those analogies which were needed to unify diversity were utilized with all seriousness. To take one of the most famous, John of Salisbury was willing to speak of the prince as the head of the body politic, the senate the heart, the court the sides, officers and judges the eyes, ears, and tongue, executive officials the unarmed and the army the armed hand, the financial department as belly and intestines, and so on.[11] But this sort of thing was a commonplace and goes back to St. Paul. More-

[11] See Otto Gierke, *Political Theories of the Middle Age*, trans. Frederic William Maitland (Cambridge, 1900), n. 76, p. 131.

over, the custom of seeing animal and human bodies in the constellations as well as envisioning the signs of the zodiac as almost identical with parts of the body must have made the strange analogy seem reasonable and perhaps even enlightening.

By the fifteenth and sixteenth centuries the practice of thinking of man as a microcosm was in decline, for the new science was in germ in Padua and by the sixteenth century would be in flower. The metaphor of the microcosm was treated seriously only by philosophers like Pico della Mirandola and Reuchlin, who were more given to speculative than to empirical thinking. Since the latter of these two men is the more important we shall conclude this chapter with him. His remarks on the microcosm which interest us are in his treatise *De arte cabalistica* ("On the Cabala").[12] There are, he maintains, four worlds, but what is contained in them all is contained in each of them. They are the angelic and invisible world, the celestial world, the sublunary and corruptible world, and man. There are correspondences among all the parts of all the worlds, and as man is one of the worlds, this correspondence must be found in him. To make much sense out of these correspondences is a risky task and one cannot be sure that one has succeeded, for a greater than normal sympathy with the system of the cabala is needed.

The Sephirotic Tree, which we have illustrated, may clarify portions of what Reuchlin has to say. Superior

[12] Reuchlin's *De arte cabalistica* is printed in Pico's *Opera Omnia*, Basel, 1557.

to everything is the Spirit of God. God has a spirit, the Metatron who communicates between the intellectual world, the world of eternal ideas, and the corporeal world. He is called (p. 773) "the intellectual agent of the First Mover." There is then the soul of the Messiah "of an essence continuous with both the angelic and divine world," after whom comes the soul of Elha. Pico is firm in insisting that there are no real gaps between these worlds and, we might add for ourselves, there are no gaps in our souls, according to classical theory, between the reason, the will, and the memory, which are simply names for different functions of the one soul. In the *Heptaplus*, Reuchlin is a bit clearer. There he has only three worlds, the intellectual, the celestial, and the corruptible, that is, the world of Platonic ideas, the heavens with their stars and planets, and the sublunary world. These, he says (p. 61),

> stand for the three parts of a man . . . at the top his head, then that which extends from his neck to his navel, third that which extends from his navel to his feet. . . . It is wonderful how beautifully, how precisely by the most exact formula they correspond in proportion to the three parts of the world. There is in the head the brain, source of knowledge; in the chest the heart, source of vital motion and heat; there are in the male the outer genital members, principle of generation. So also in the world there is the uppermost part which is the angelic or intellectual, the source of knowledge because that nature [the angelic] was made for understanding. There is a middle part, which is the heaven, principle of vital mo-

tion and heat, in which the sun dominates as the heart in the chest. Below is the Moon, that is known to all as the principle of generation and corruption. Moses, however, designated the first by the proper name of the head; the second, however, he called fire, because the heaven is thought of by this name by many people, and because in us this part is the principle of heat. The third he called the fundament, because by it the whole body of man, as is known to all, is founded and sustained.

Pico adds to this that there exists between the parts of the body and the world a treaty of friendship and concord, "so that the whole world is one in itself and also is one with its supreme author."

One can see that the notion of self-knowledge equaling knowledge of the whole might be justified in Pico's picture of the four worlds. But we shall stop here, for we have illustrated how a figure of speech expands to become the foundation of a set of ideas much wider than its original. From the beginning, in Plato, of thinking of the human body as consisting of the same four elements as the whole world and therefore resembling the whole world, we arrive, in Pico, at a detailed description of the world in terms of human psychology. The use of the metaphor did not stop here, but this was about as far as its extension went. We could cite the *Microcosme* of Maurice Scève (1511-64), where the term is used only of Adam before the Fall, or Shakespeare's use of the allegory of the belly (in *Coriolanus*, i.1) and the revolt against it, which goes back to Livy via Plutarch, but enough has been said to accomplish our purpose.